DEDICATION

This book would not be possible without the wonderful support of my family. From my parents, Robert Sr. and Penny Sellers, who have made our travels possible by helping my wife and I acquire our motorhome. To my loving wife, Amanda that works many hours volunteering with me at State Parks to earn our stay; as well as play housekeeper, and mother to our daughter, Savannah. This book is also dedicated to her, and my two sons, Zachary and Robert III (Robby).

Special thanks to my friend Xavier Bruehler, author of When the Fault Breaks for his support.

PREFACE

I am a certified professional photographer, born and raised in Pasadena, Maryland. In 2010, my wife and I decided to take life on the road. We purchased our first motorhome, and just days later we found out there would be an addition to our family. Our first road trip was to Savannah, Georgia. We loved the city so much; we aspired to return someday and named our little girl Savannah Hope.

After five years on the road, (and several returns to Savannah) we ended up returning to Anastasia State Park in St. Augustine, Florida, where we volunteered in 2012. Although Savannah has a special place in our hearts, we're certain St. Augustine is where we will settle when we stop traveling.

The photos included in this book are shots from around St. Augustine from our three months stay at Anastasia State Park, February to April 1st, 2015. I've included some stories and history, but the main goal of this book is to showcase my photography.

Click HERE to visit the Traveler's Pics home page where you will find links to my "Museum Quality Gallery" and "Zazzle Store" for products adorned with images from my gallery. Or, visit http://travelerspics.us.

The city was beautifully adorned for the holidays upon our arrival on February 1st. We were fortunate to have the opportunity to catch the attraction. The following day, the decorations were taken down.

There is some legend behind this particular canon we found online. Town historians were unable to confirm the information. Online sources alleged this canon (#29) was on board North Carolina Privateer Brig Bellona when it ran aground on December 2nd, 1780 just south of Anastasia Island.

Several of the privateers on board the ship, including Captain Gilbert Harrison, Lewis Dishon, and John Dishon (brother of Lewis) were captured by the British. This was all a great interest to us, as Lewis Dishon is my wife's 6th great grandfather.

However, the canon is stamped as Civil War era.

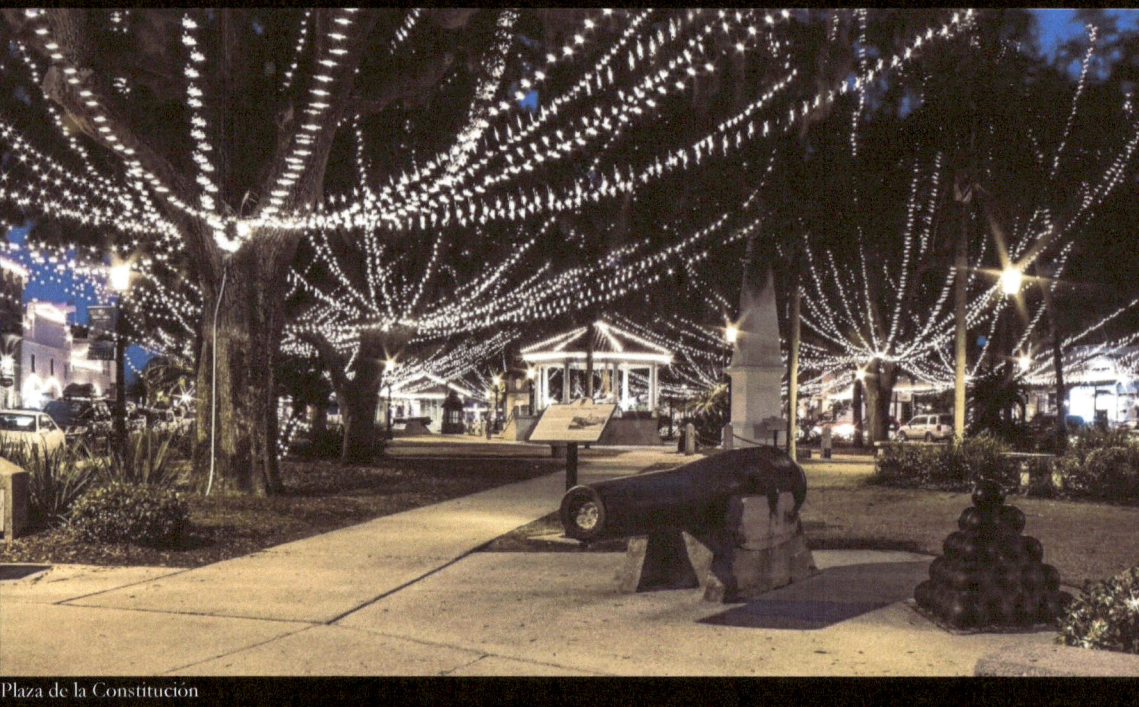

Plaza de la Constitución

The story goes that there were several survivors of the Bellona's wreck. Five of the men, including Captain Harrison, Lewis, and John were captured by the British and subsequently held at Castillo de San Marco.

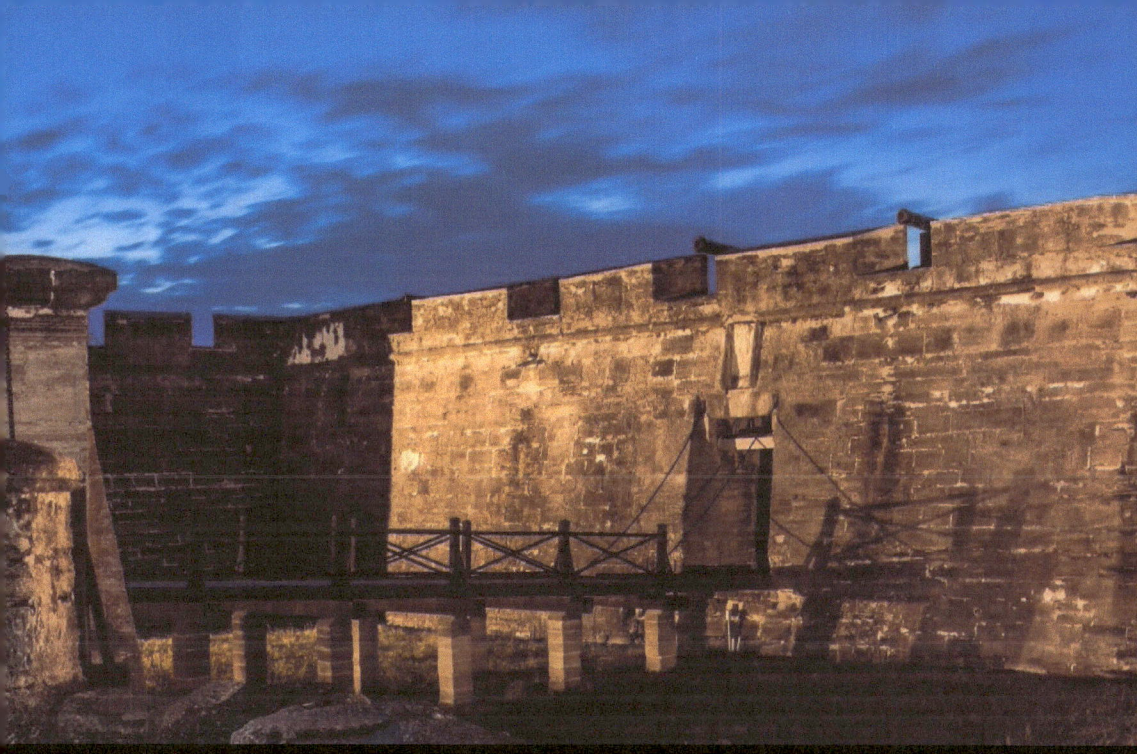

Entrance to Castillo de San Marcos

May 5th, 1782 Lewis, John, their Captain, and two other prisoners managed to escape the fort.

"... and four more men of the crew made their escape -- and were about 20 or 22 days in the wilderness. While in the wilderness, the declarant & his comrades got on the track of the cattle, which one McGirt, a robber, had taken from Georgia to St. Augustine for the British. He discovered the track of a cow that had got away from McGirt's drove & was returning towards Georgia; & he & his men pursued it & finally overtook her & made beef of a part of her -- which perhaps saved their lives -- as they were nearly starved. At length, they reached Ogeechee, the edge of the white settlement, & thence made their way home where they arrived the latter part of June 1782." - Pension Application of Lewis Dishon

There are no clues as to how the men managed to escape the fort.

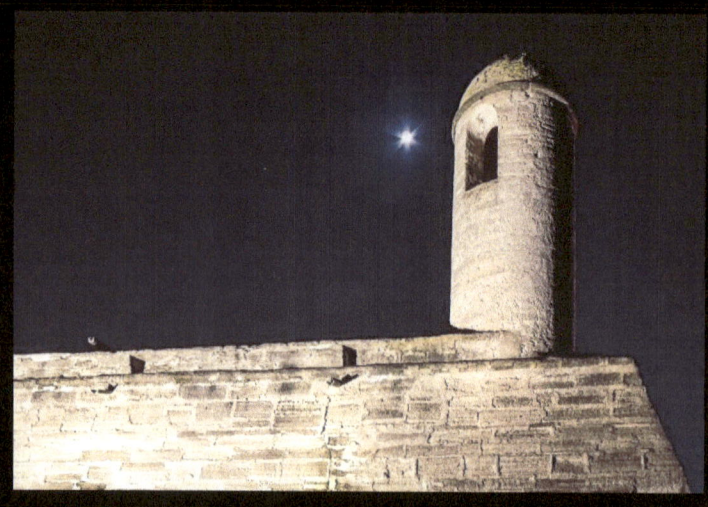

Construction of the fort began in 1672 by order of the Governor of "La Florida" Francisco de la Guerra. Spanish engineer, Ignacio Daza was responsible for its design.

St. Augustine became the British capital of East Florida in 1763 after the signing of The Treaty of Paris. Castillo de San Marcos was then renamed Fort St. Mark.

After the American Revolution, in 1783, the Spanish regained control of the fort.

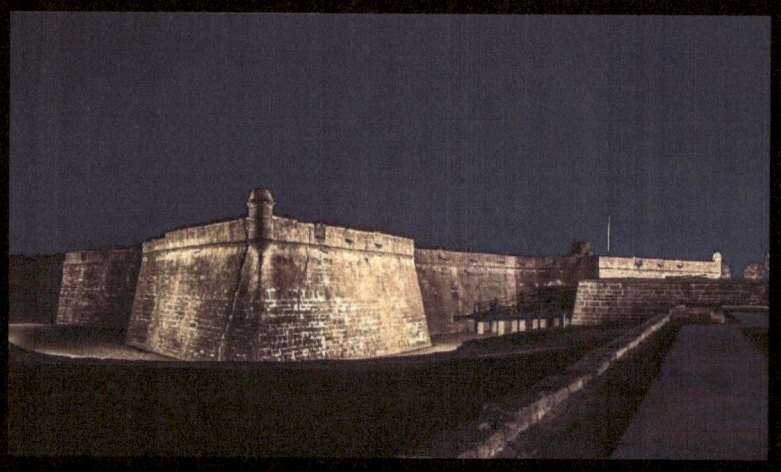

In 1819, the Spanish relinquished control of the fort to the U.S., and it was renamed, Fort Marion.

In 1924, Fort Marion was declared a National Monument. In 1942, by an act of congress, Castillo de San Marcos original name was restored.

Castillo de San Marcos National Monument was constructed from coquina quarried from Anastasia State Park. Coquina is comprised of ground up sea sediment that has hardened over millions of years. It is an outstanding material for building, and many buildings in town were constructed from coquina quarried from Anastasia Island. Coquina also has a cushioning effect that can absorb the energy of a cannonball. Instead of crashing through a wall, the cannonball would be caught like a BB in Styrofoam.

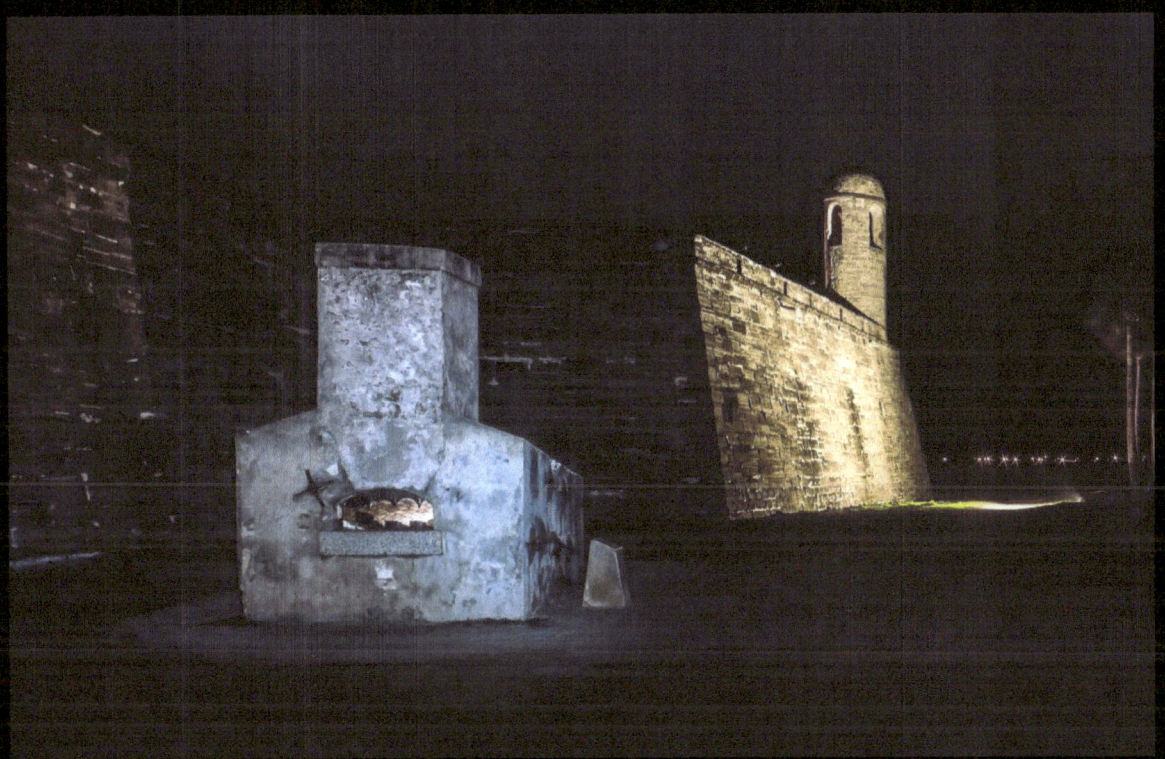

If you have never been behind Castillo de San Marco at night, it is incredibly dark. Getting this photo took some time and effort. I placed a diffused flash inside the furnace to give a fiery effect. My wife stood behind the furnace with another off camera flash and used it to flash the back wall multiple times during a 45-second exposure. At the same time, I used a small spotlight to "paint" the front and side of the furnace.

This "shot furnace" was used to heat cannonballs to be fired at enemy ships in hopes of catching their craft on fire.

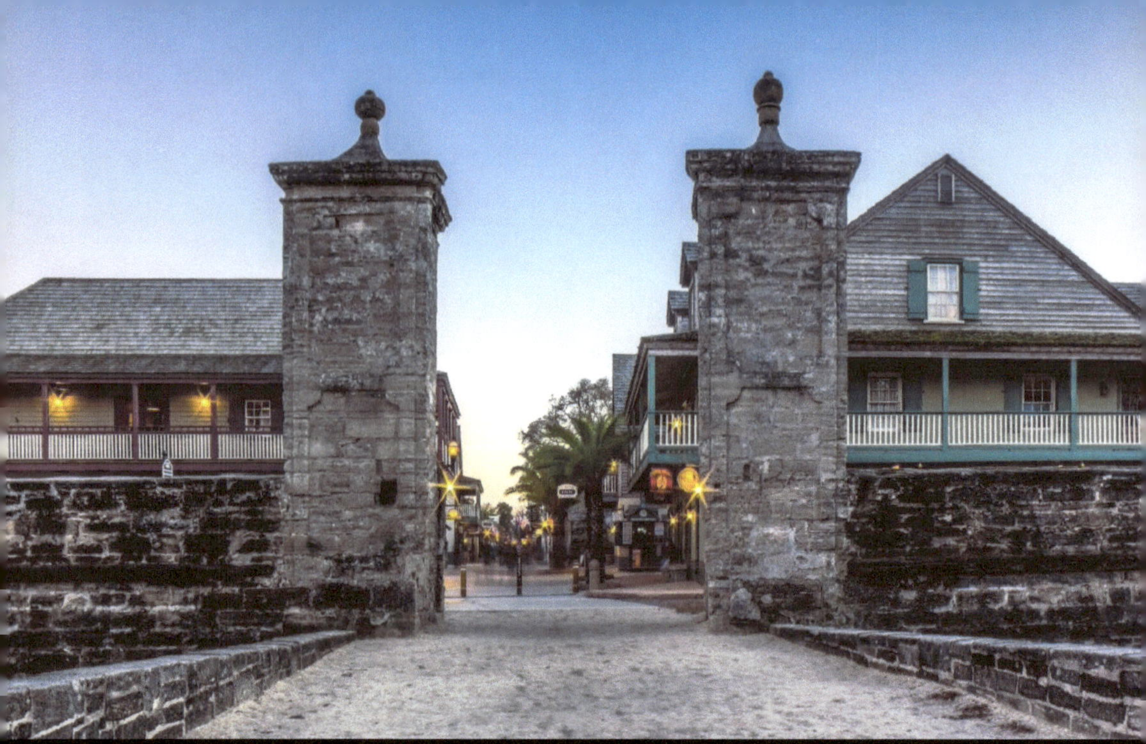

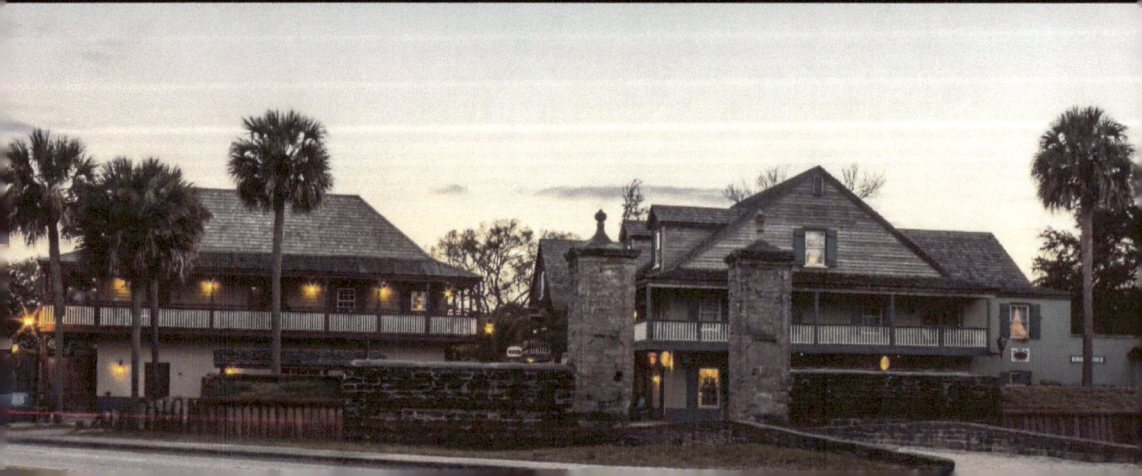

"The City Gates" is the portal to St. George Street. The "Cubo Line" was built in 1704 in response to 150 years of looting pirates. A British attack in 1702 was the last straw for the Spanish. The City Gate was the only entrance to the City. From what we were told by a tour guide, they were closed at dusk, and if you were not back in town by the time the doors were shut, there was no getting back in. The last time the Cubo Line was used to protect the city was during the Second Seminole Wars, 1835-1842.

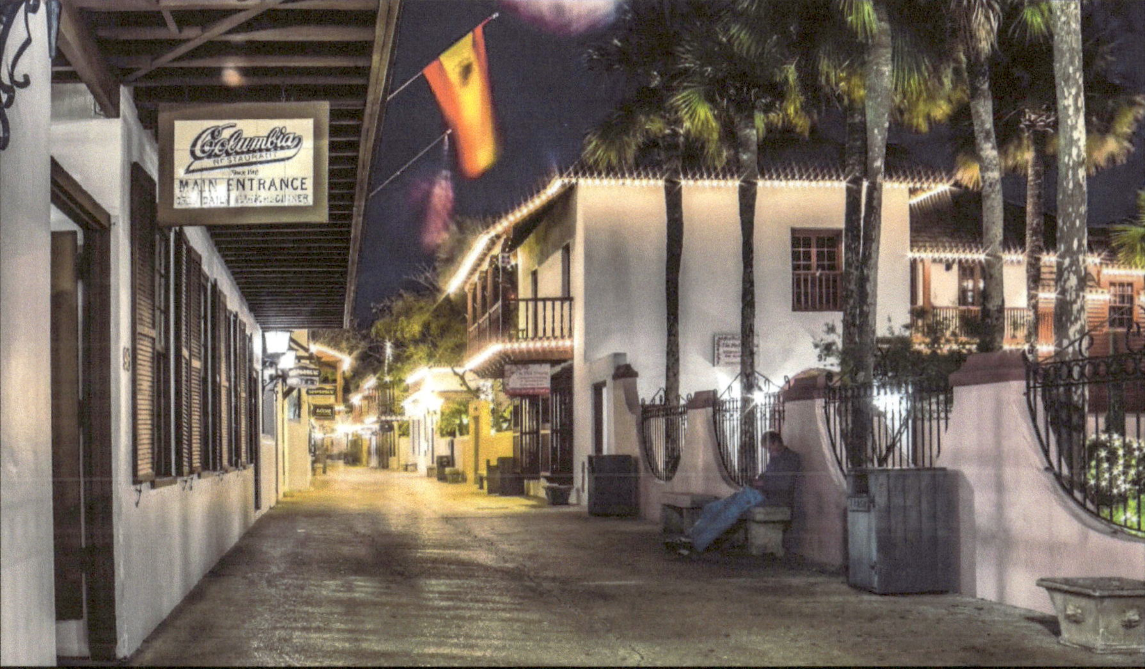

A few streets in the United States claim to be the oldest, but I almost have to take St. Augustine's word on this one. Archeologists have found clay pots that date back to the 1600's, which has Philadelphia's oldest Elfreth's Alley from 1702 beat. They have also discovered ashes that may date back to 1586 when Sir Frances Drake burned St. Augustine to the ground.

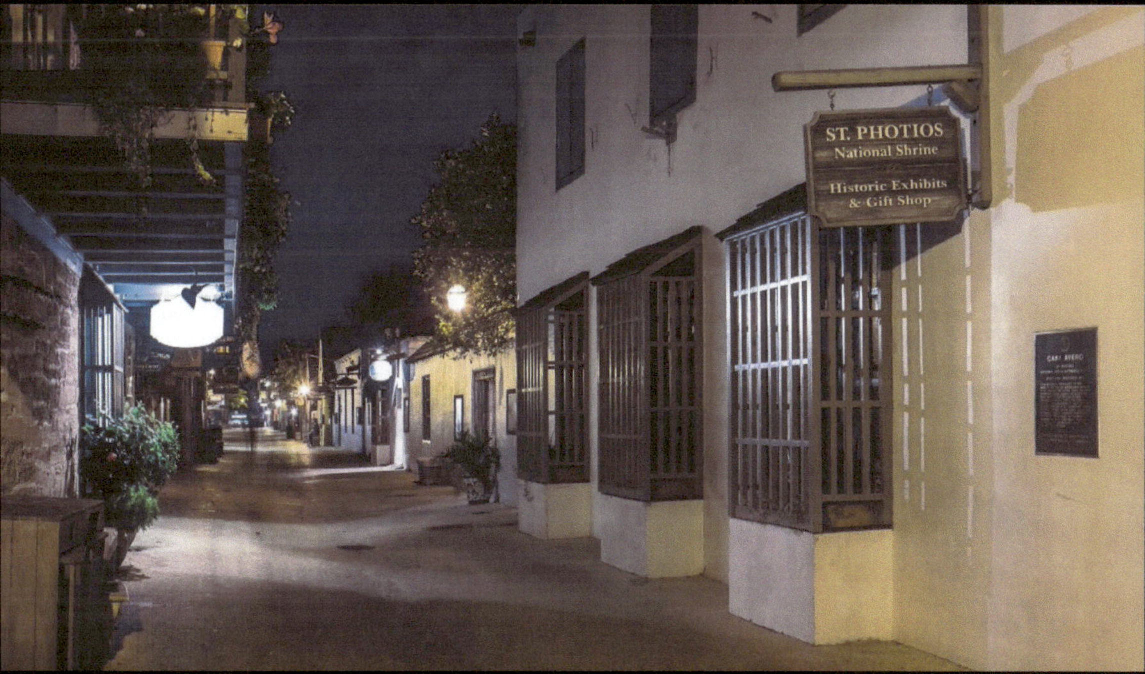

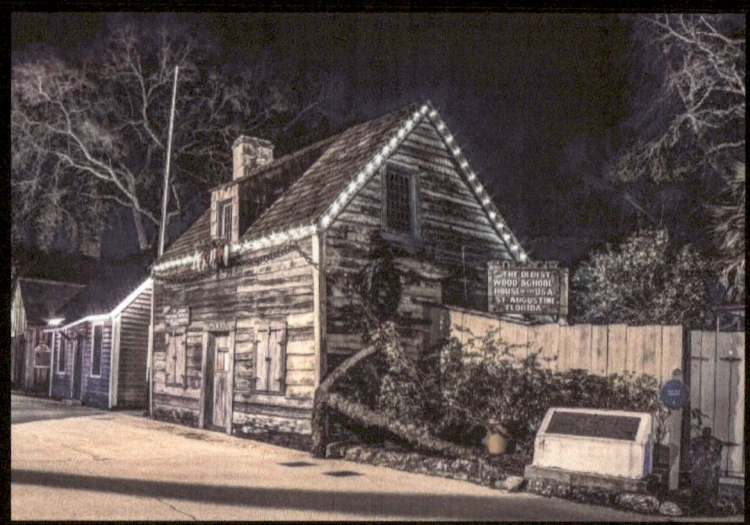

St. Augustine is also home to The Oldest Wooden Schoolhouse in the U.S. The oldest schoolhouse was constructed over 200 years ago. During its operation, a schoolmaster lived above the small classroom.

Like most wooden homes of the time, the kitchen was not part of the dwelling. This was done to prevent house fires. The house was constructed of cedar, which was common practice due to cedars ability to keep insects at bay.

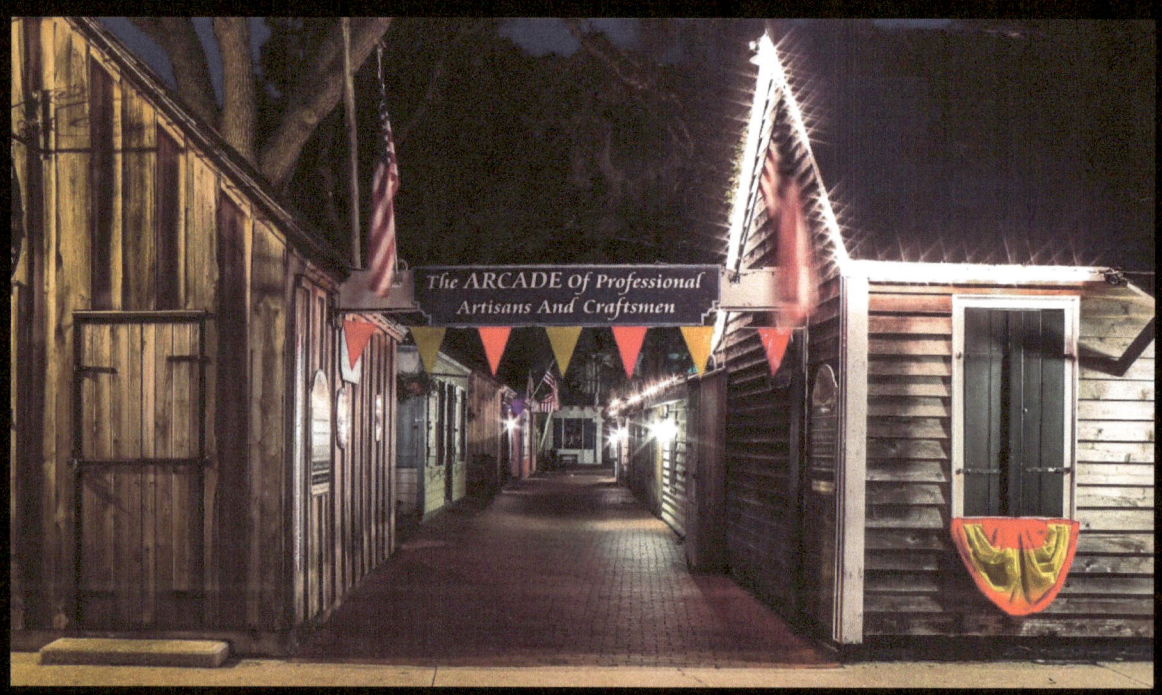

St. Augustine is a city full of art. You will find galleries throughout the city.

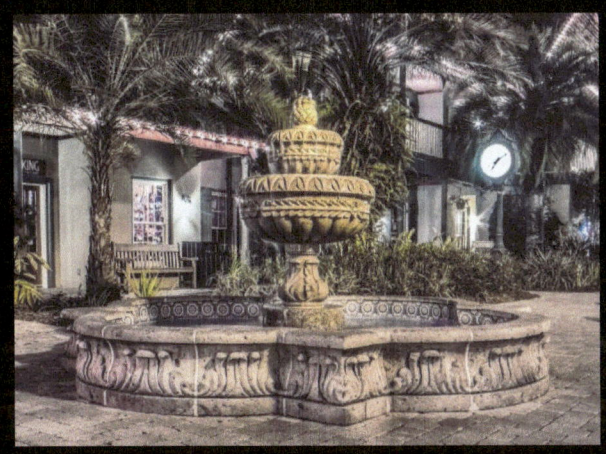

I was unable to find anything regarding the history of this fountain, but it was nice nonetheless. It is nestled in a small square just off the beginning of St. George Street at Tolomato Lane. We were happy to see that it had been restored since vandals destroyed it near the end of our 2012 visit to the city.

I just can't go on without the special mention of our favorite place in town to grab a bite. We met the owners of Burger Buckets when we visited in 2012. At the time, it was just Fudge Buckets, and they had just opened their doors. In just a few short years their business exploded, and there's no doubt why.

They closed the original Fudge Buckets due to their need to expand and moved into this awesome little castle with the Red Train Tours. They also have a small Fudge Bucket shop right on St. George Street.

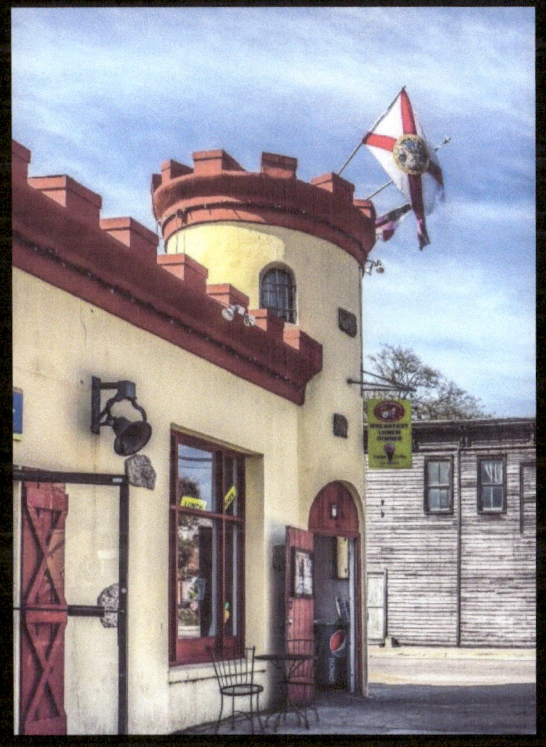

The gray wooden building in the background is The Old Drugstore; at least, it used to be. When we visited in 2012, it was a small store with homemade soaps and such. They had preserved an incredible amount of detail to make it appear authentic. It has since been transformed into a wax museum, which was quite a disappointment.

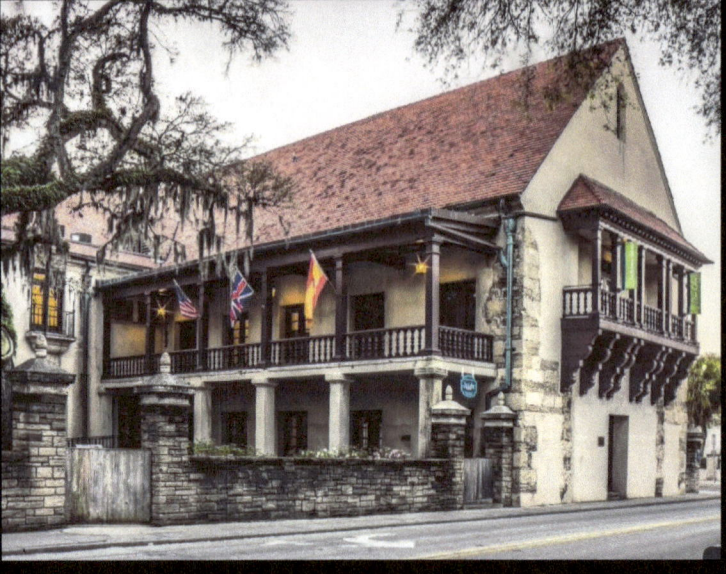

This coquina built home served as the Governor's house from 1710 through 1811. It was home to governors through both Spanish periods, and the British period that separated them.

The Government House is now a museum; attained by the State of Florida in 1964.

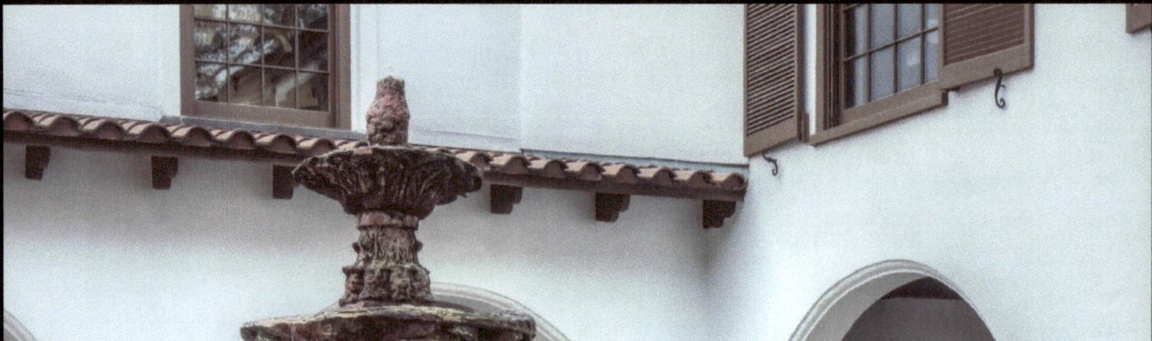

The courtyard of Columbia restaurant, established in 1905.

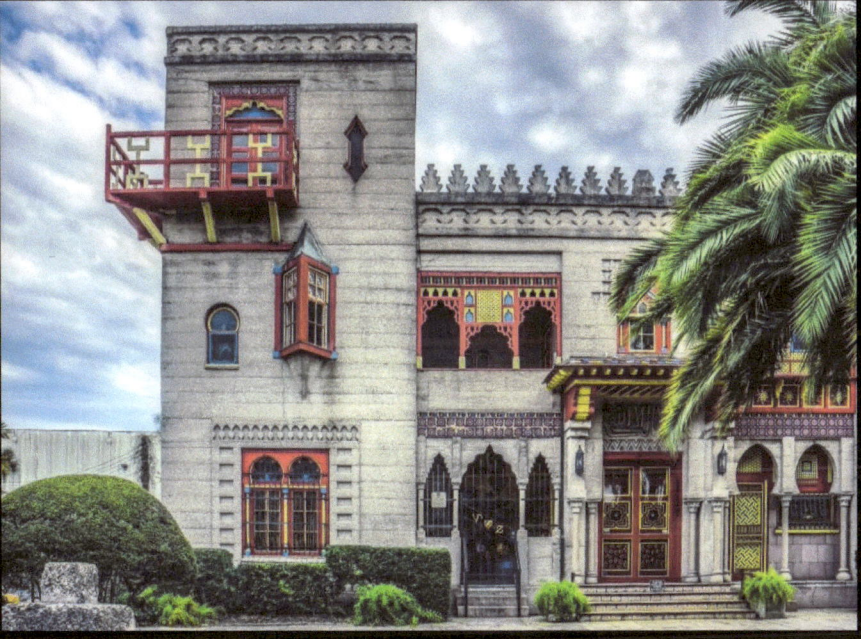

Villa Zorayda was modeled after 12th century Moorish Alhambra Palace.

Built as a home to armature architect Franklin W. Smith in 1883.

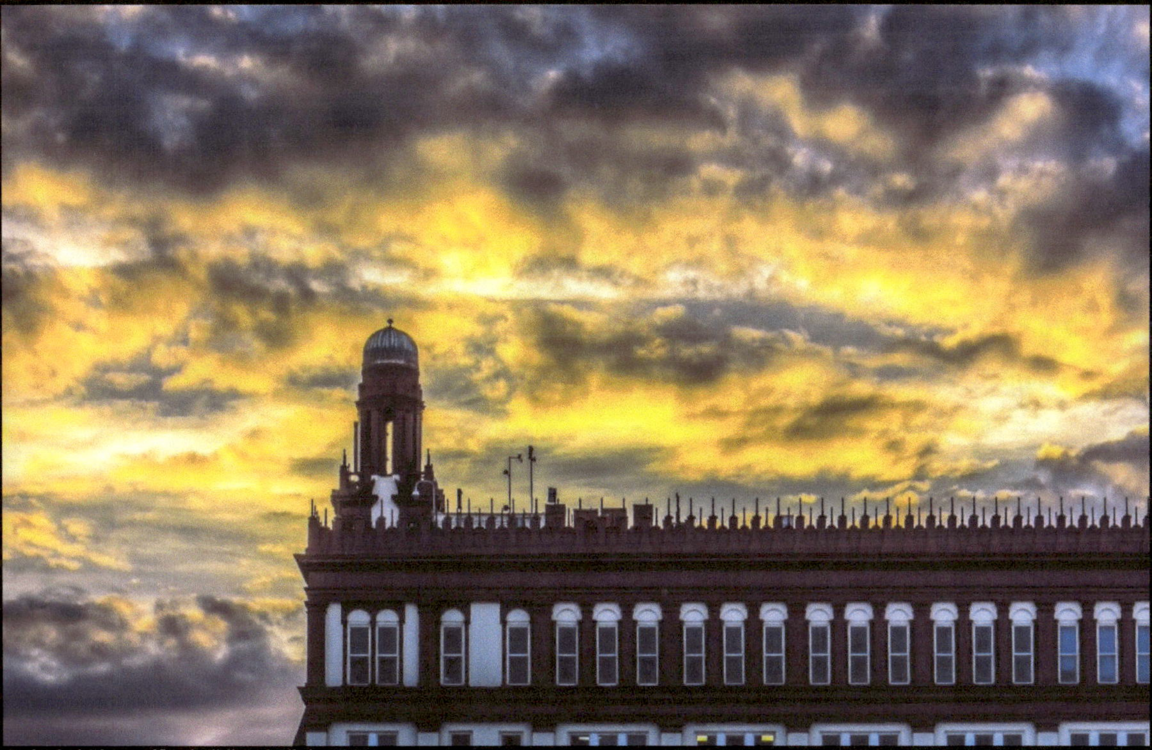

Cathedral Place office building, built in 1928.

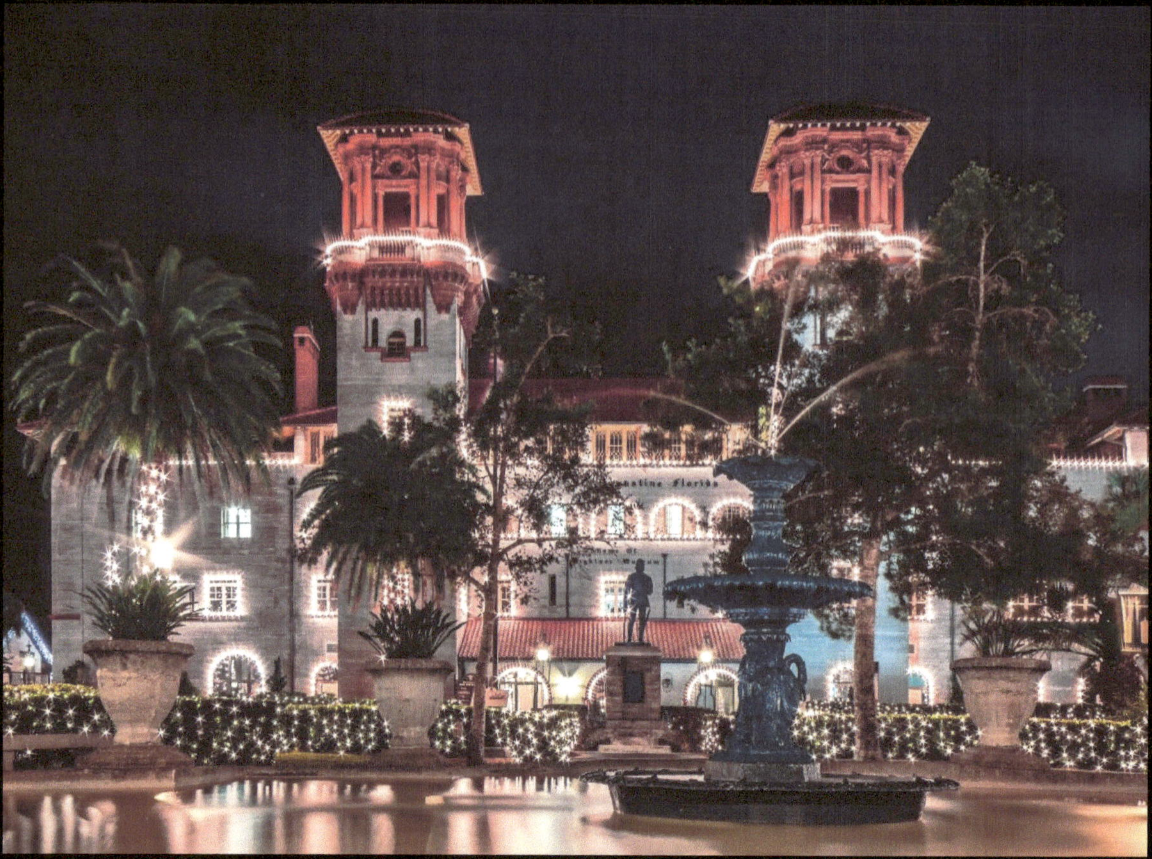

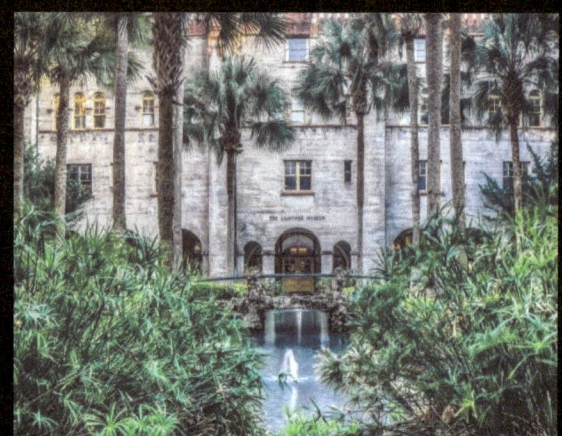

Formerly known as the Alcazar Hotel, The Lightner Museum was built in 1887. It was converted into a museum in 1948. The museum features antiquities from America's Gilded Age 1870-1900. The entire town is decked out with over 2 million lights for the holiday season.

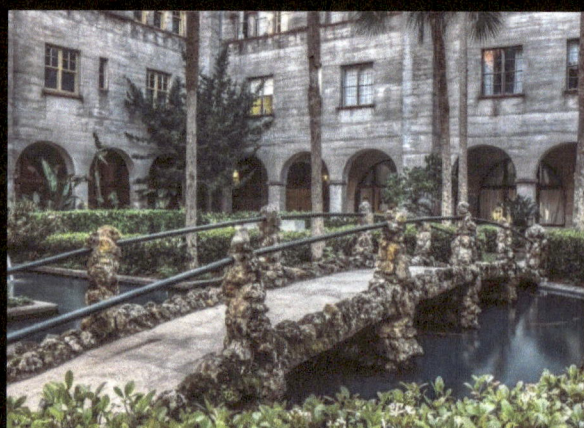

Pictured above, the courtyard of The Lightner Museum.

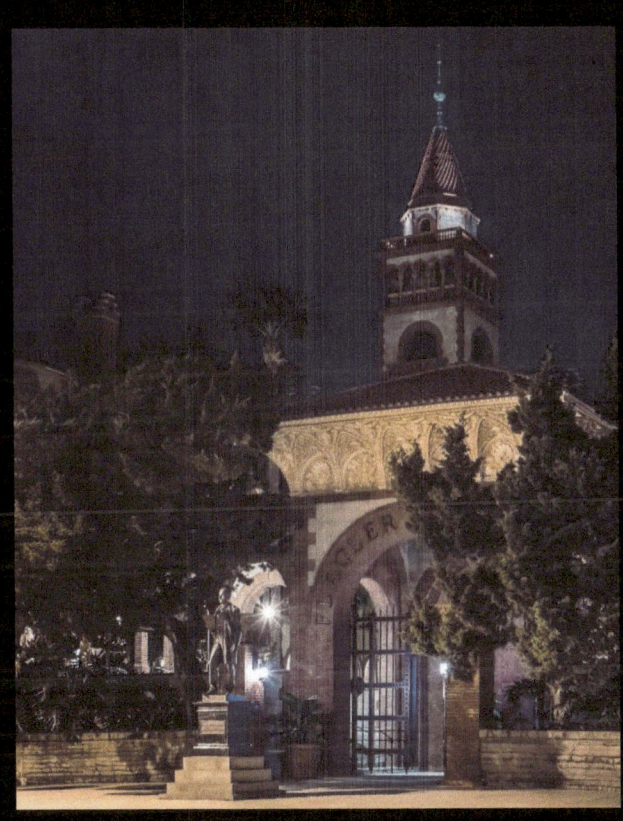

Flagler College, formerly known as Ponce de León Hotel was constructed in 1888. The building was converted into a college in 1968.

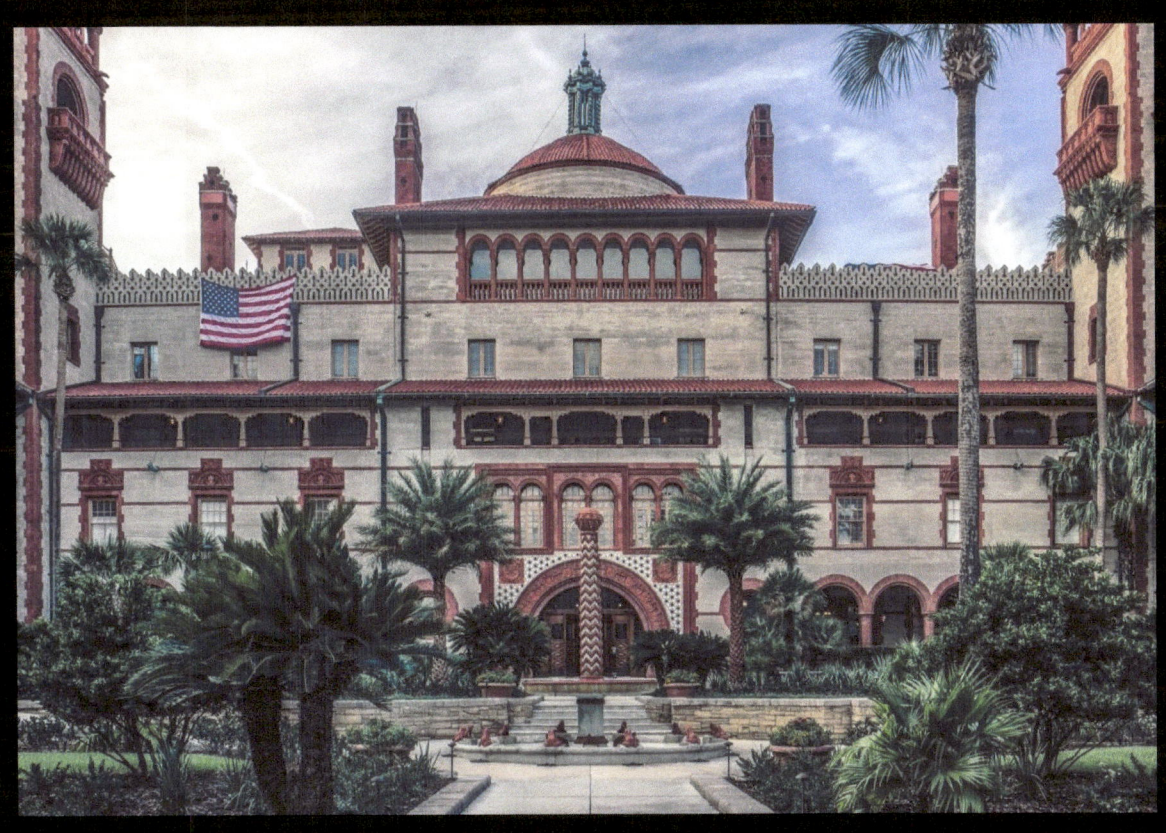

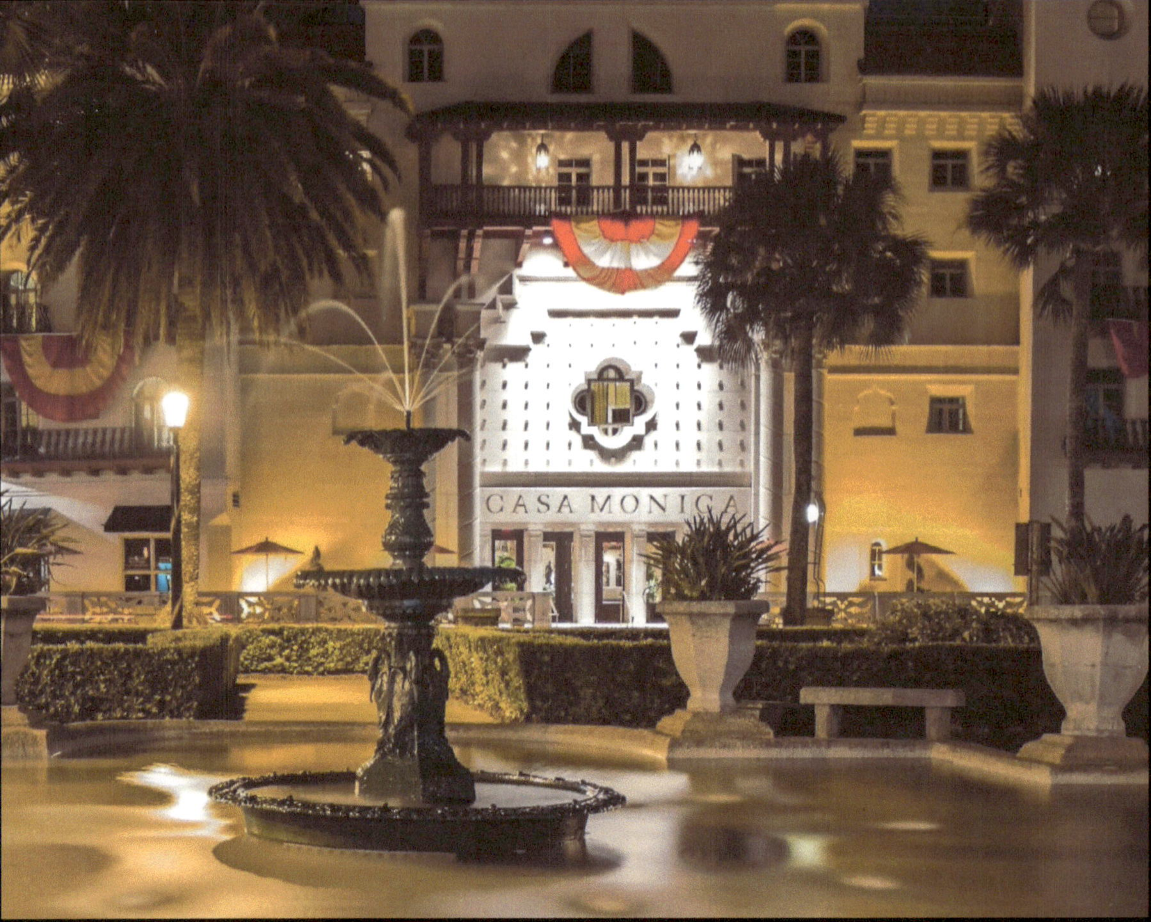

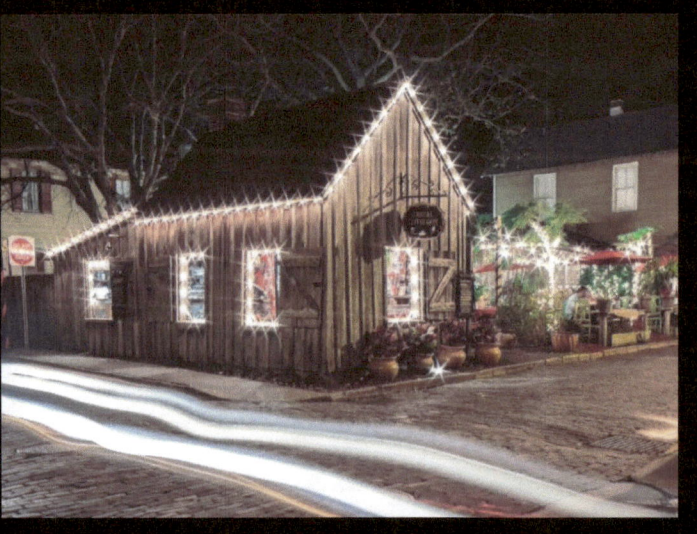

The Casa Monica was constructed by Franklin W. Smith in 1988. Due to financial struggles, Smith sold the hotel to Henry Flagler, who renamed the hotel to The Cordova.

This photo of The Crucial Coffee Café was achieved with a long exposure. The streaks of light at the bottom left were a passing car.

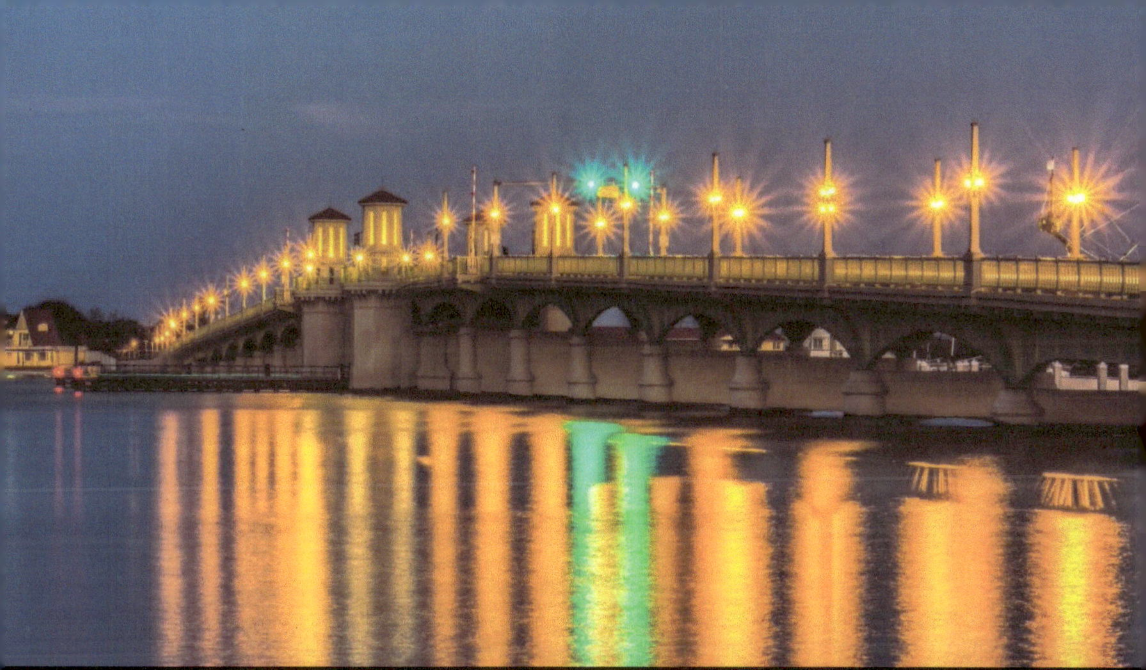

The Bridge of Lions was completed in 1927 and spans the Matanzas Bay.

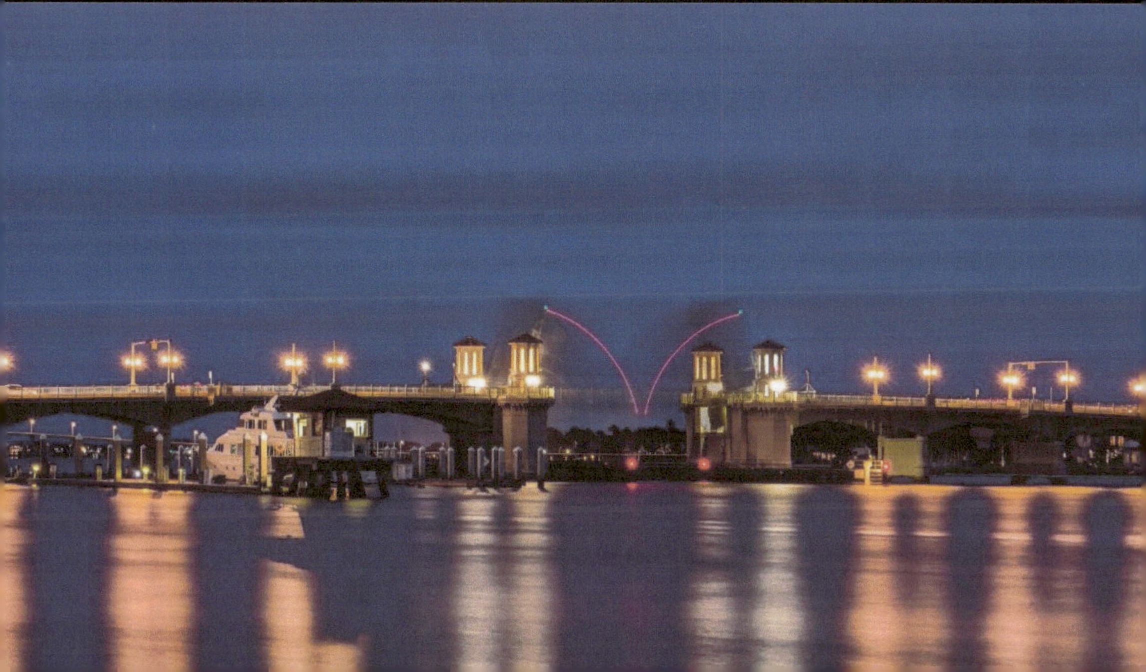

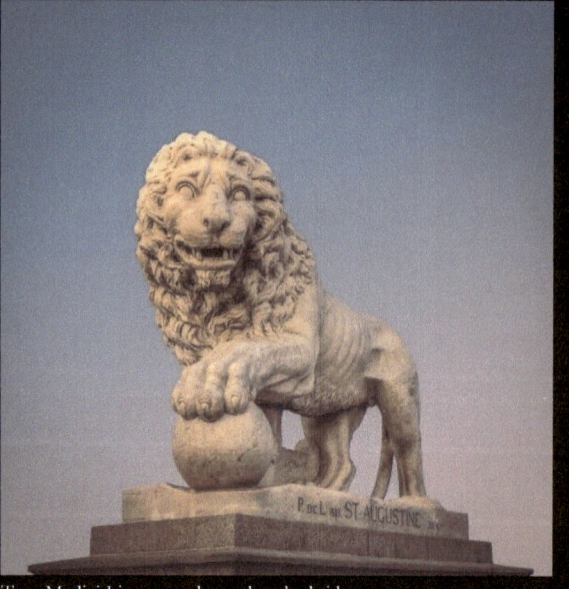

Two Medici Lions stand guard at the bridge entrance.

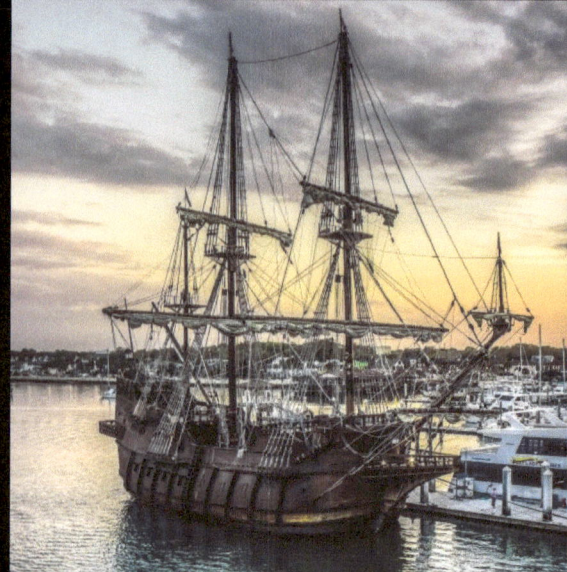

El Galion docked by The Bridge of Lions

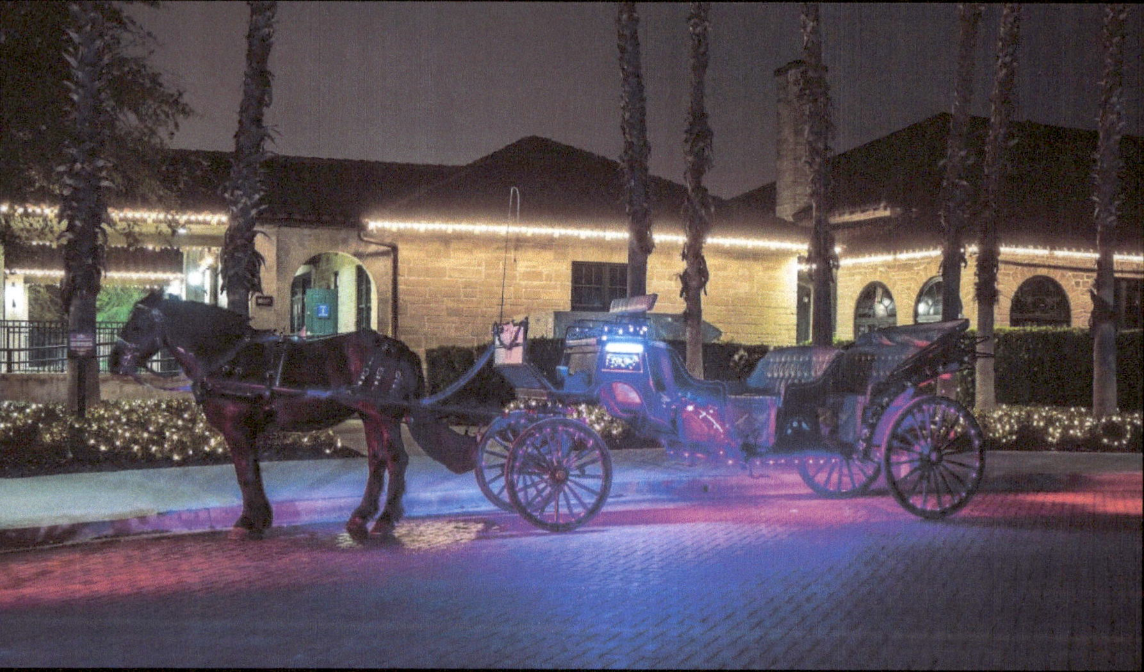

One of many horse-drawn carriages that provide tours throughout the city.

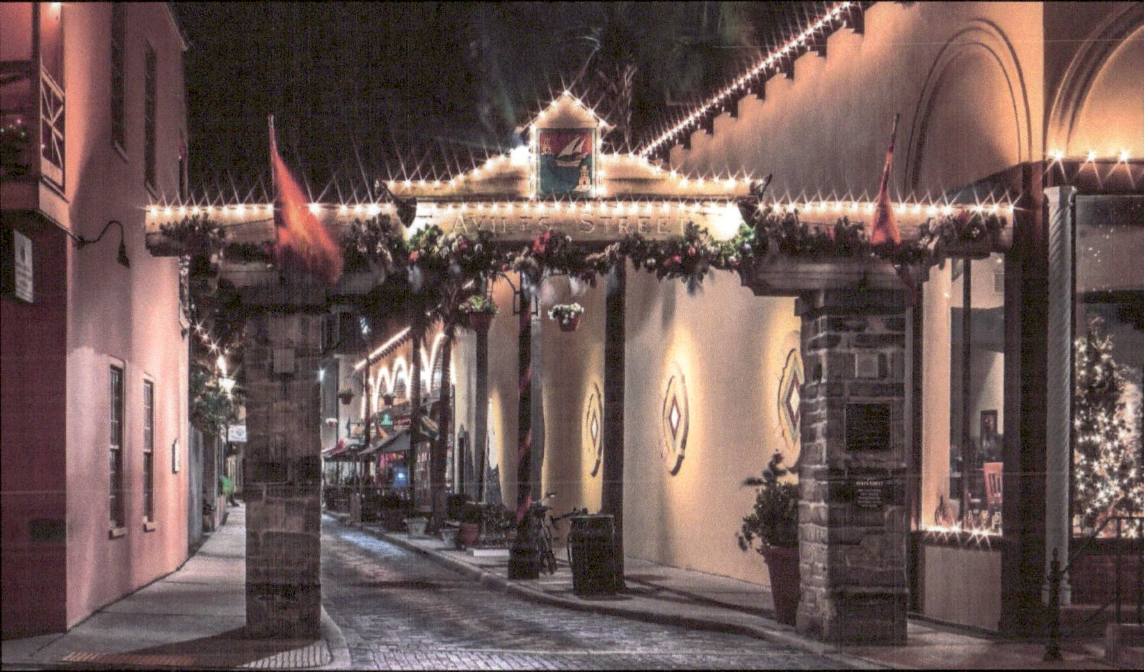

The beginning of Aviles Street during Christmas

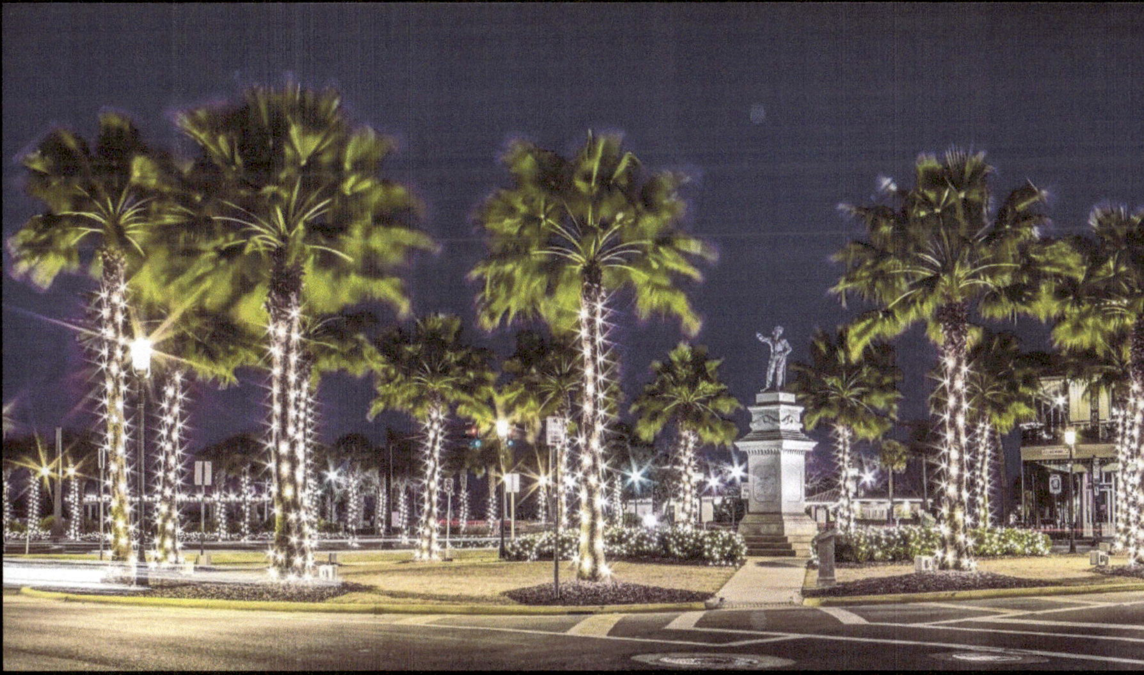

Juan Ponce de Leon's statue stands at his actual height 4'11". The statue was donated to the city by Dr. Andrew Anderson in 1923.

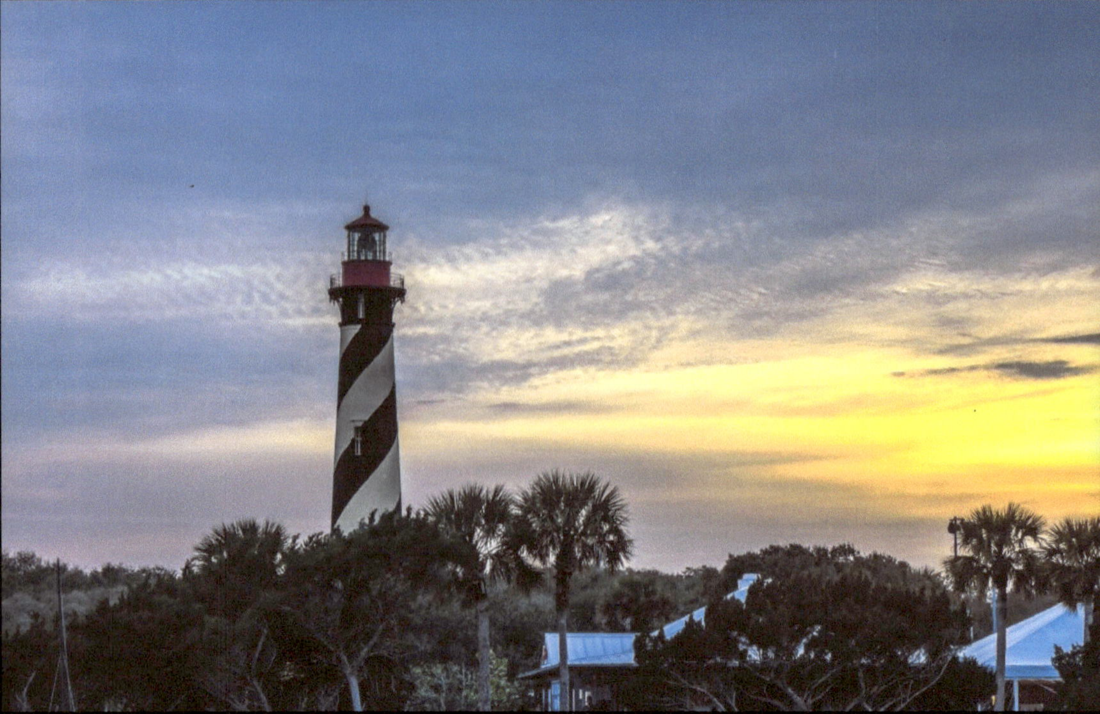

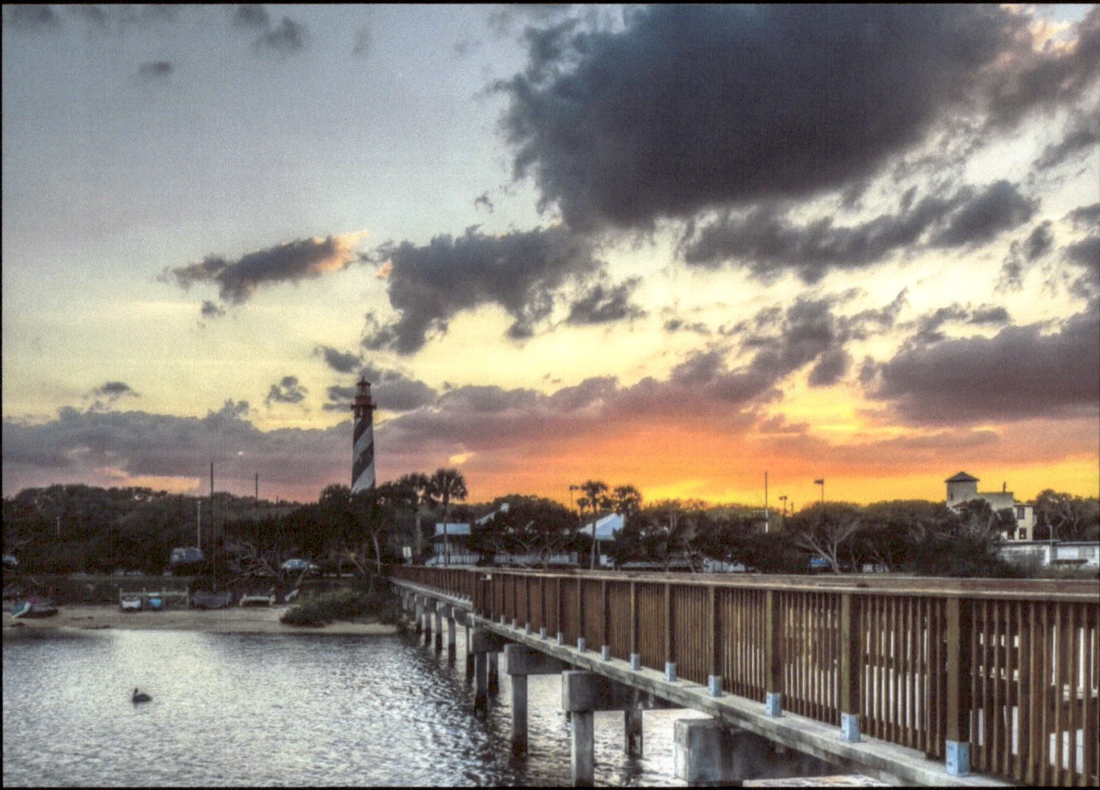

St. Augustine Lighthouse & Museum was built in 1874

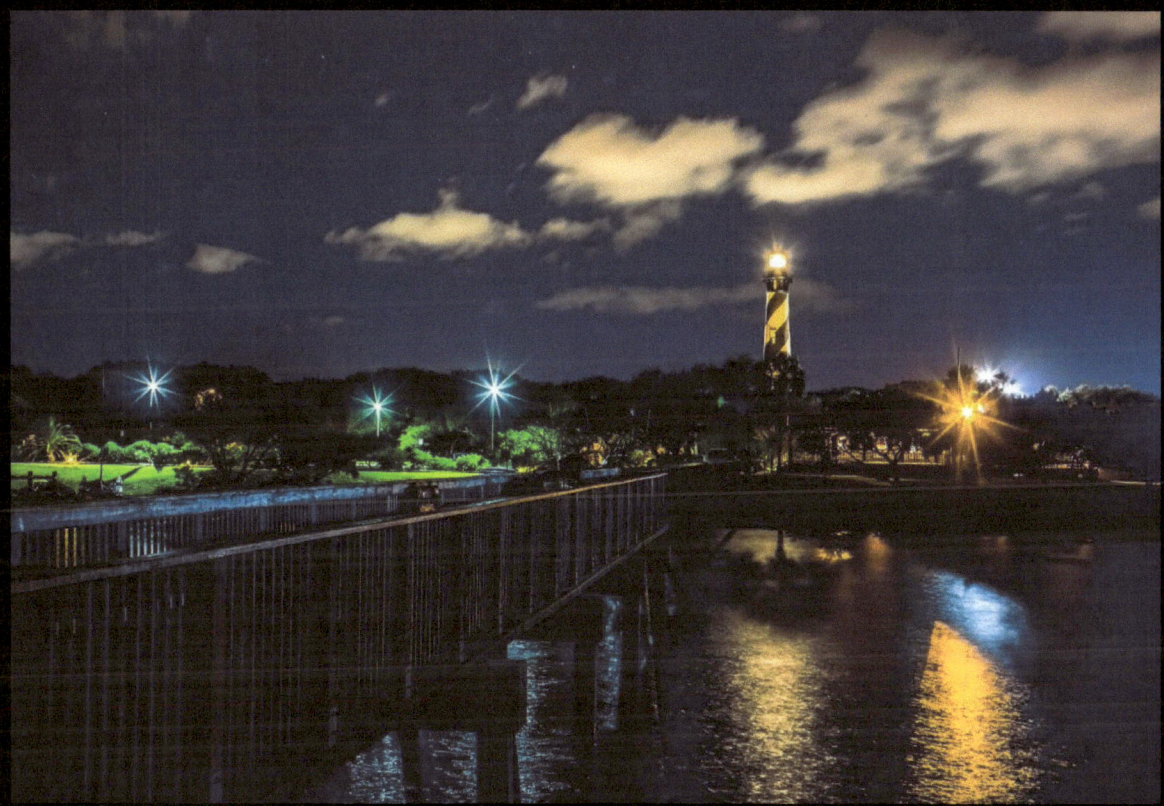

St. Augustine Lighthouse & Museum at night.

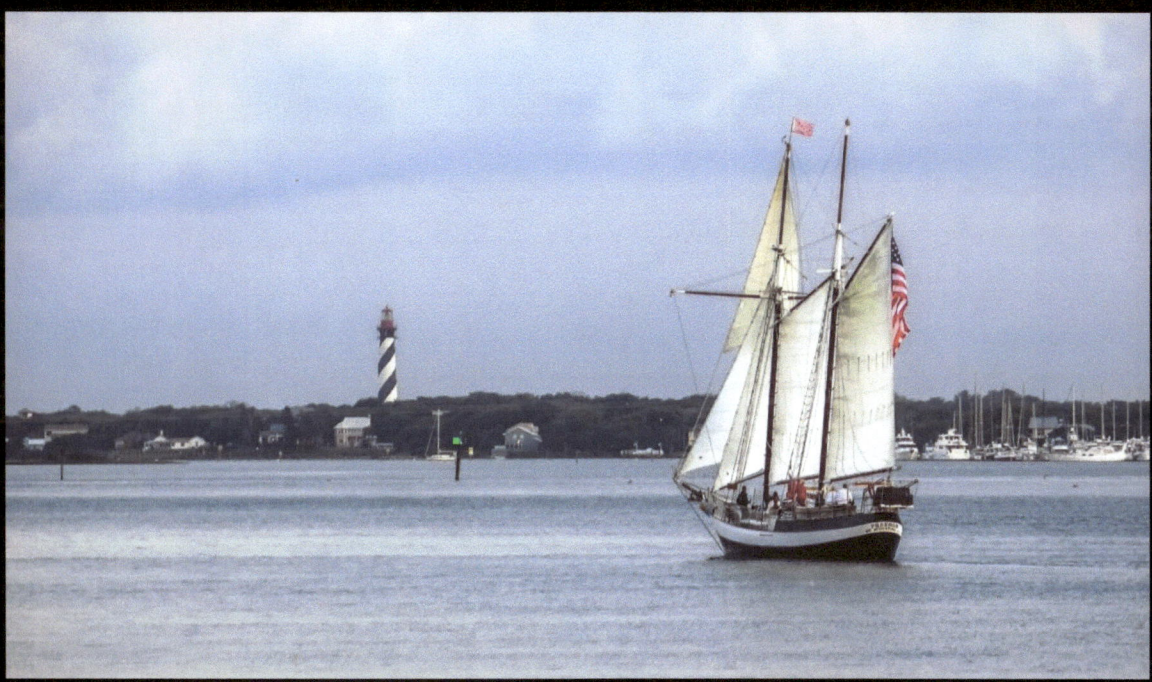

Schooner "Freedom" nearing St. Augustine Lighthouse & Museum.

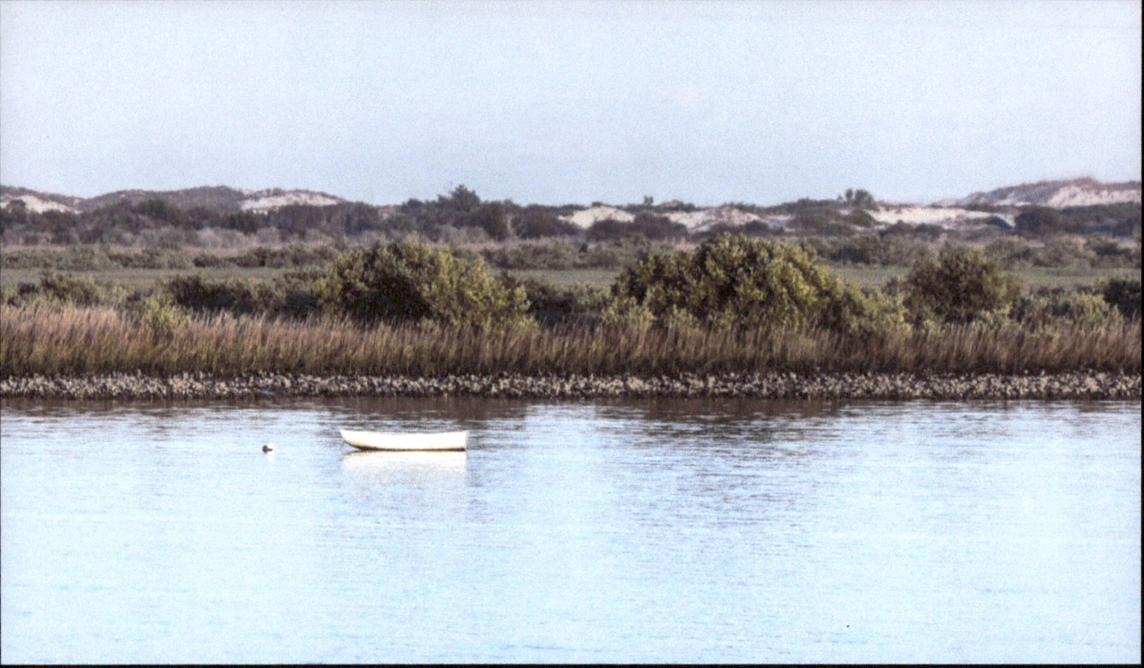

Images of "Salt Run" from the pier across from St. Augustine Lighthouse.

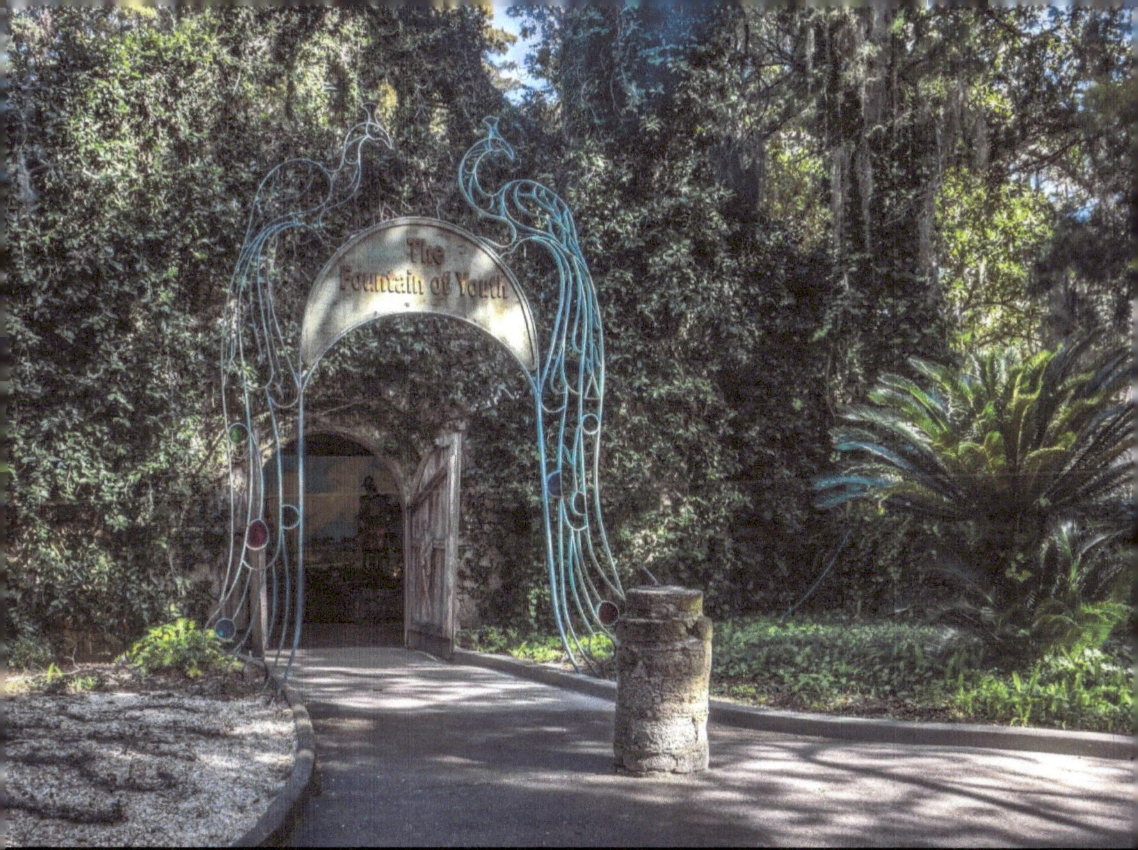

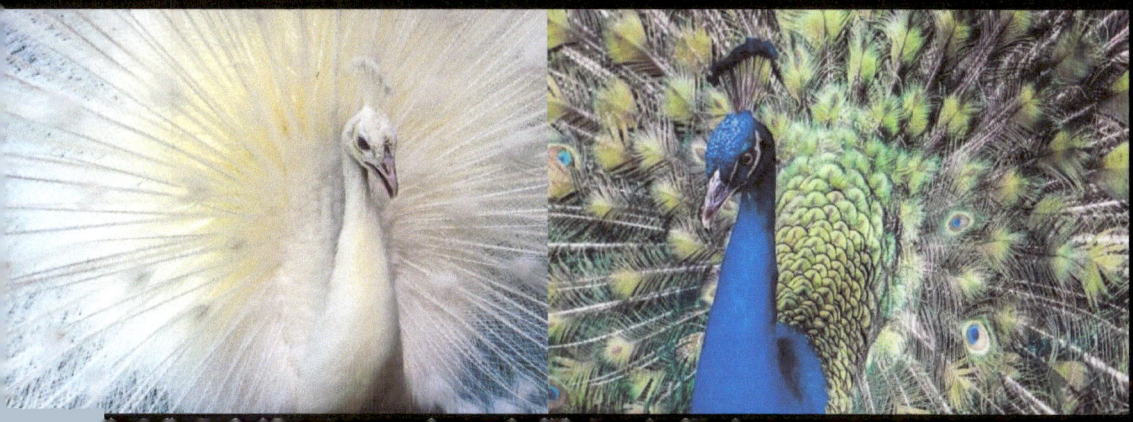

Ponce de Leon's Fountain of Youth Park

Inside this building is the actual fountain from the legend of Ponce de Leon's Fountain of Youth. There is no documentation that Ponce de Leon ever really came in search of a Fountain of Youth. He instead came in search of gold. The legend of the fountain may have stemmed from the longevity and height of the local natives. Ponce de Leon himself was only 5'3 with his extra tall hat.

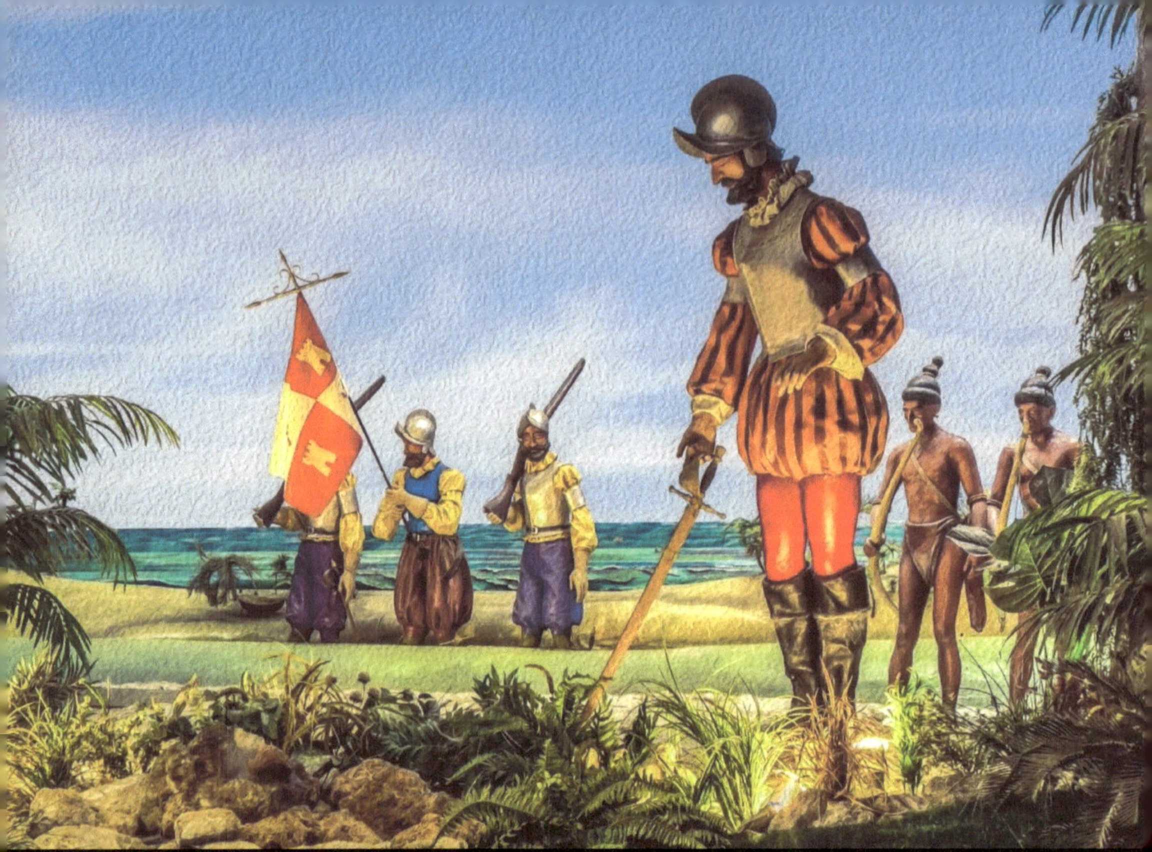

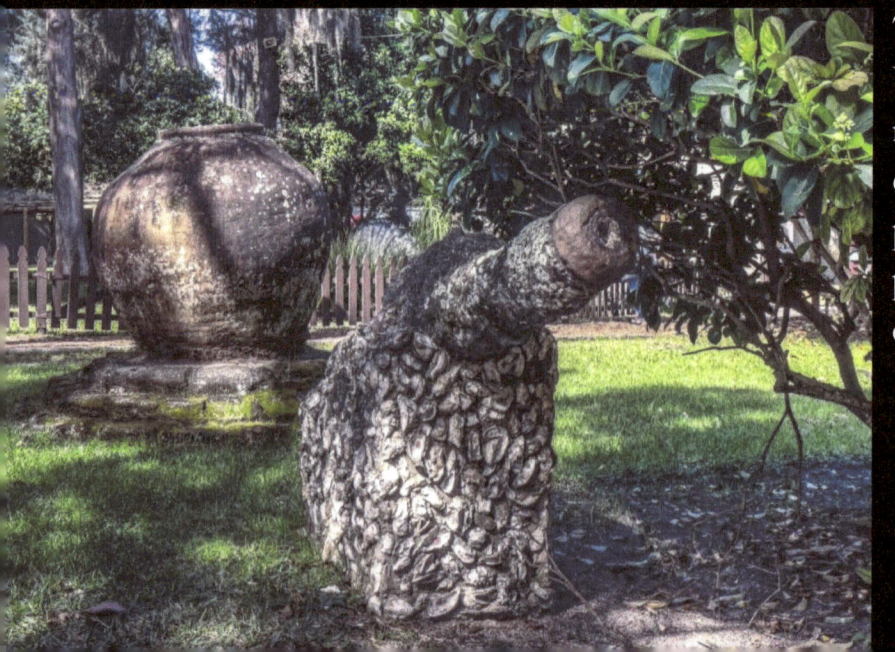

Ponce de Leon at the Fountain of Youth in digital oil painting.

The Fountain o
Youth Park was
much bigger than
expected. It is a
place you can
plan to spend the
day.

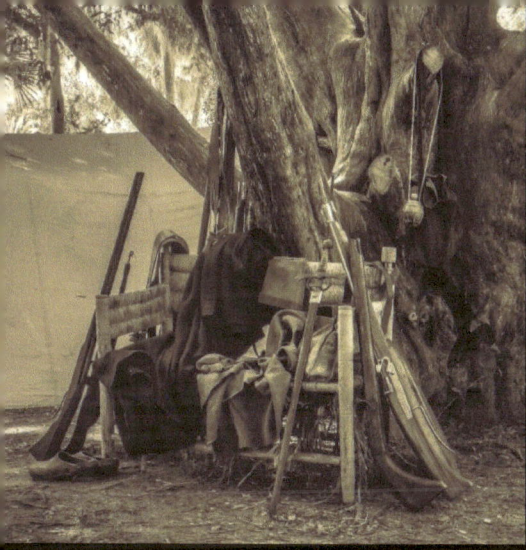

In 1687, the Spanish government of Florida began to offer asylum to slaves who fled the British colonies.

In 1738, Fort Mose was established as a free black settlement.

James Oglethorpe of Georgia led the Siege of Fort Mose. Although the fort was destroyed, Oglethorpe returned to Georgia, as the inhabitants of Fort Mose relocated into St. Augustine.

During Fort Mose's Flight to Freedom reenactment, Ranger Steve Gard of Anastasia State Park plays the part of Don Joseph De Leon. One of Don Joseph De Leon's jobs was to baptize the troops before battle.

For a black person to be granted their freedom at Fort Mose, they must have sworn allegiance to the King of Spain, and converted to Catholicism.

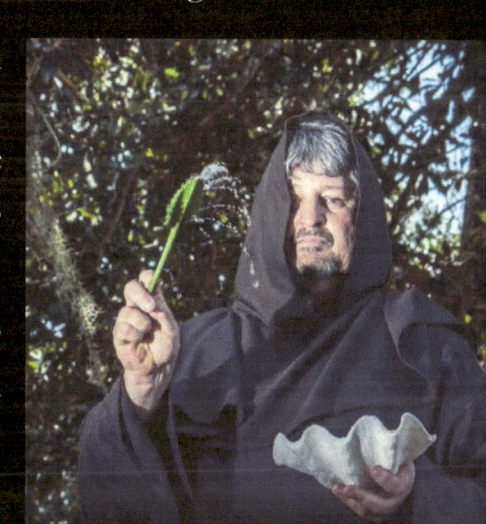

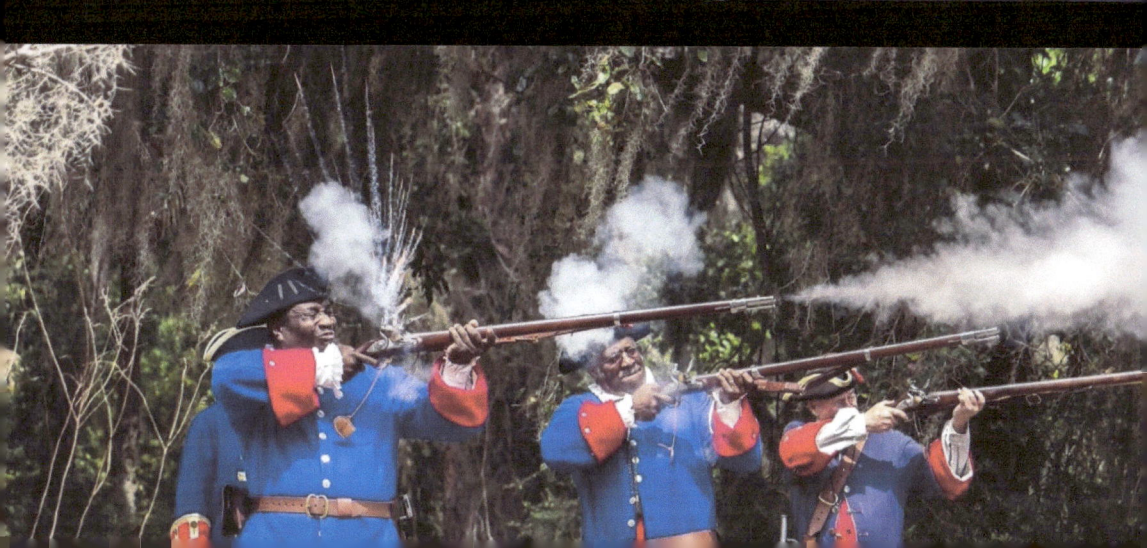

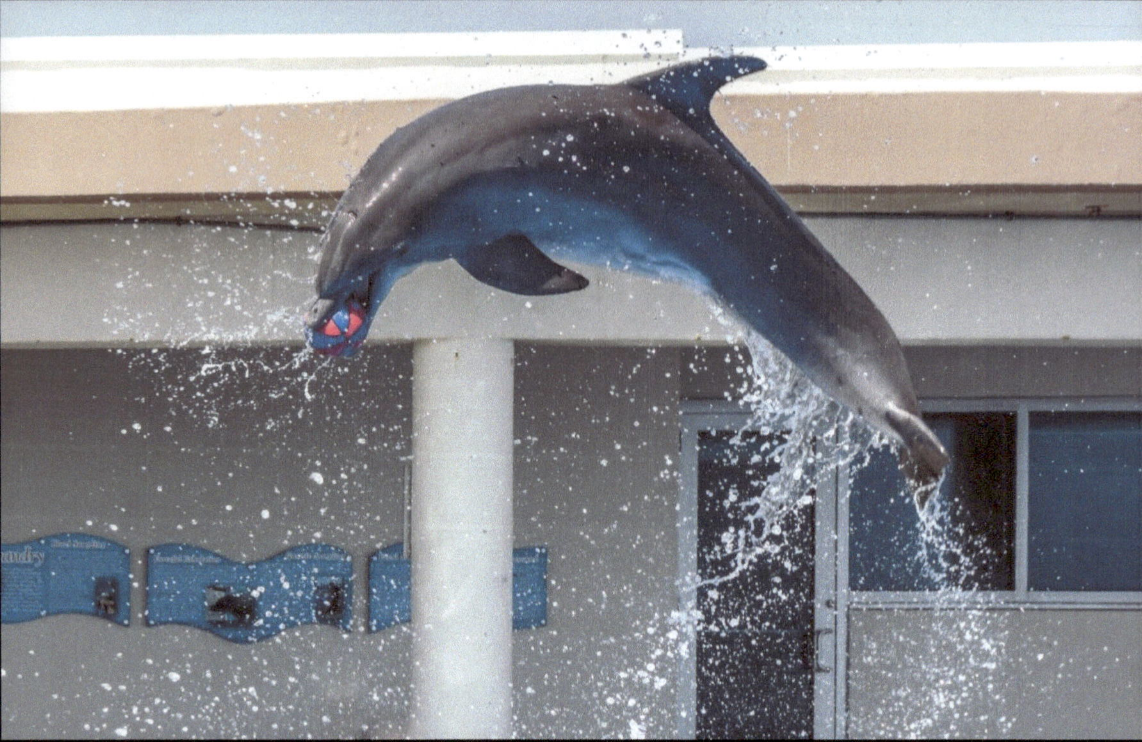

Marineland, Florida is approximately 20 minutes south of Anastasia State Park.

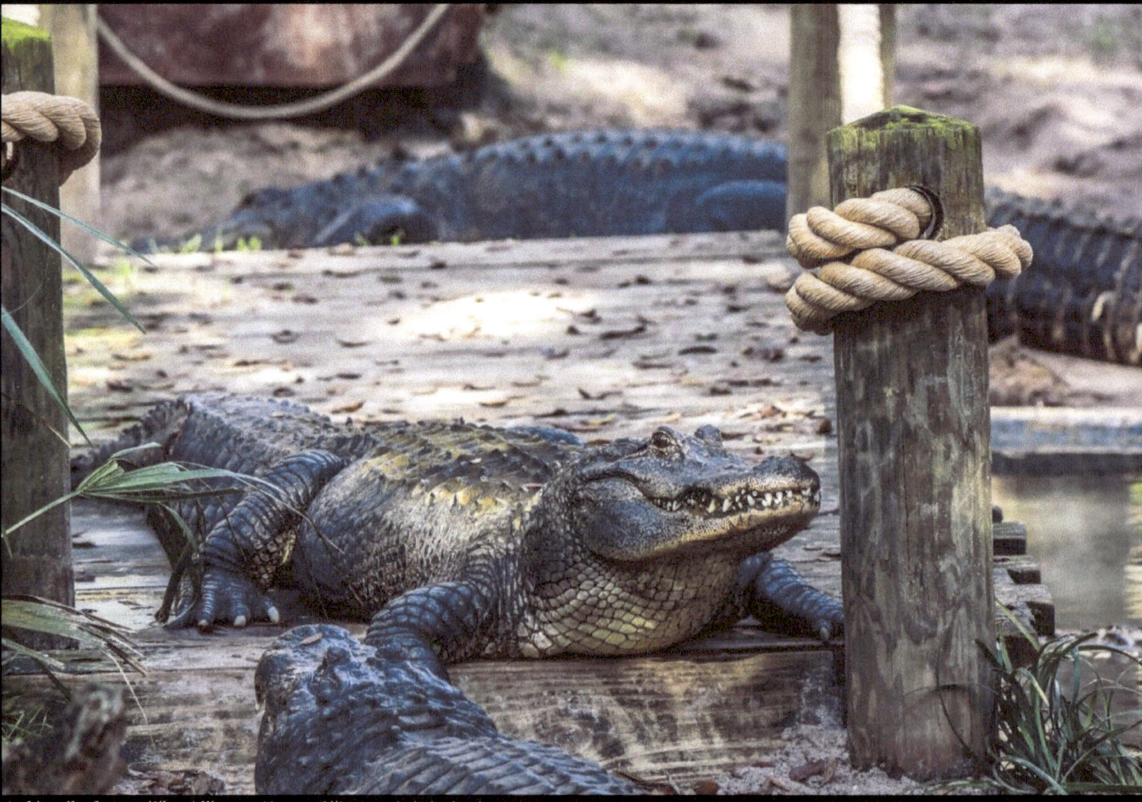

A friendly face at The Alligator Farm *Alligator mississippiensis*

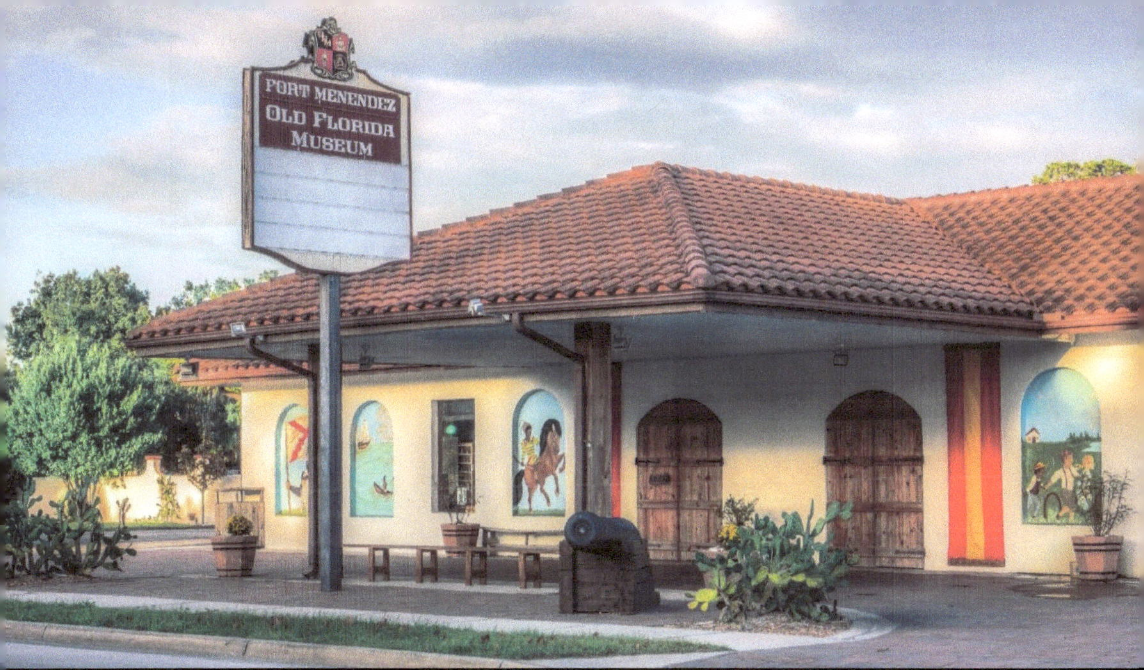

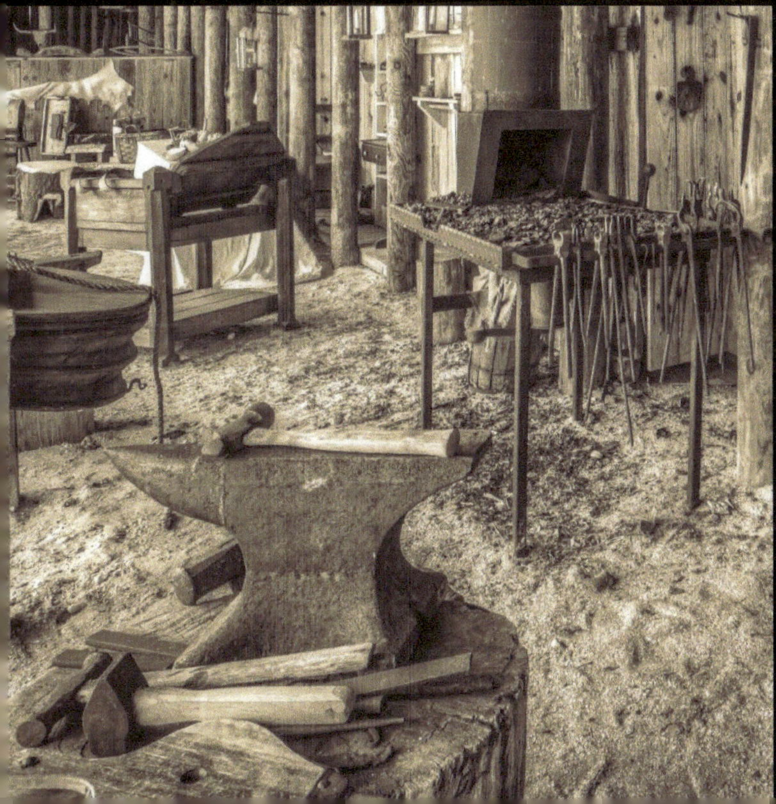

Fort Menendez at the Old Florida Museum is a great place for the kids. They have many hands on activities and demonstrations to keep them entertained and educated.

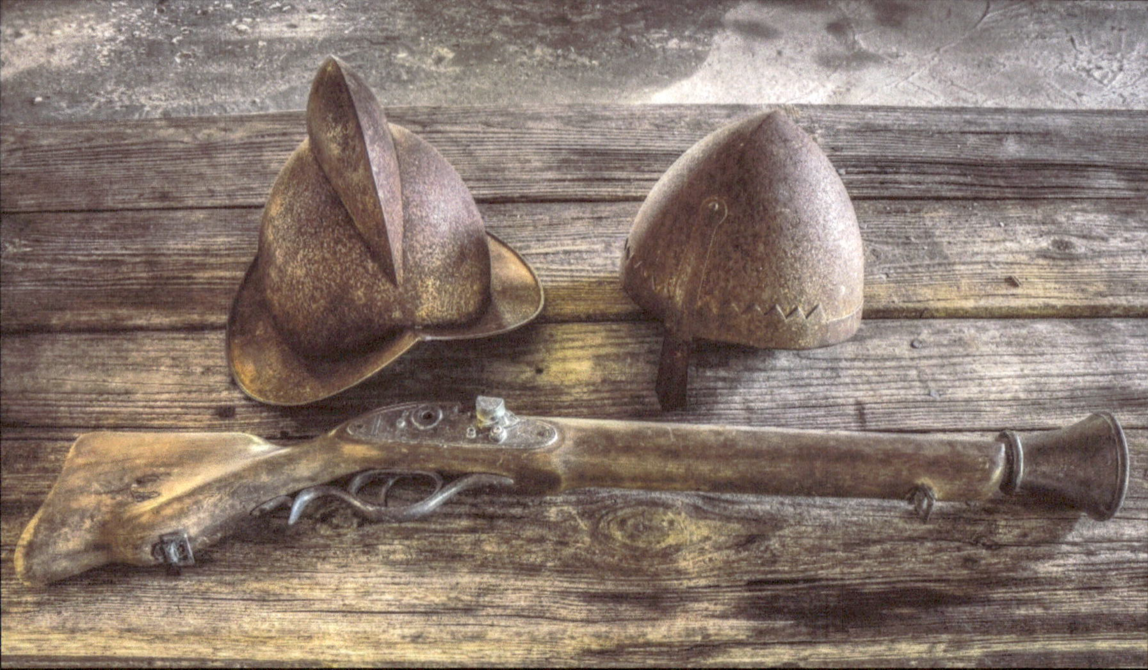

Some replica 1500's gear at Fort Menendez

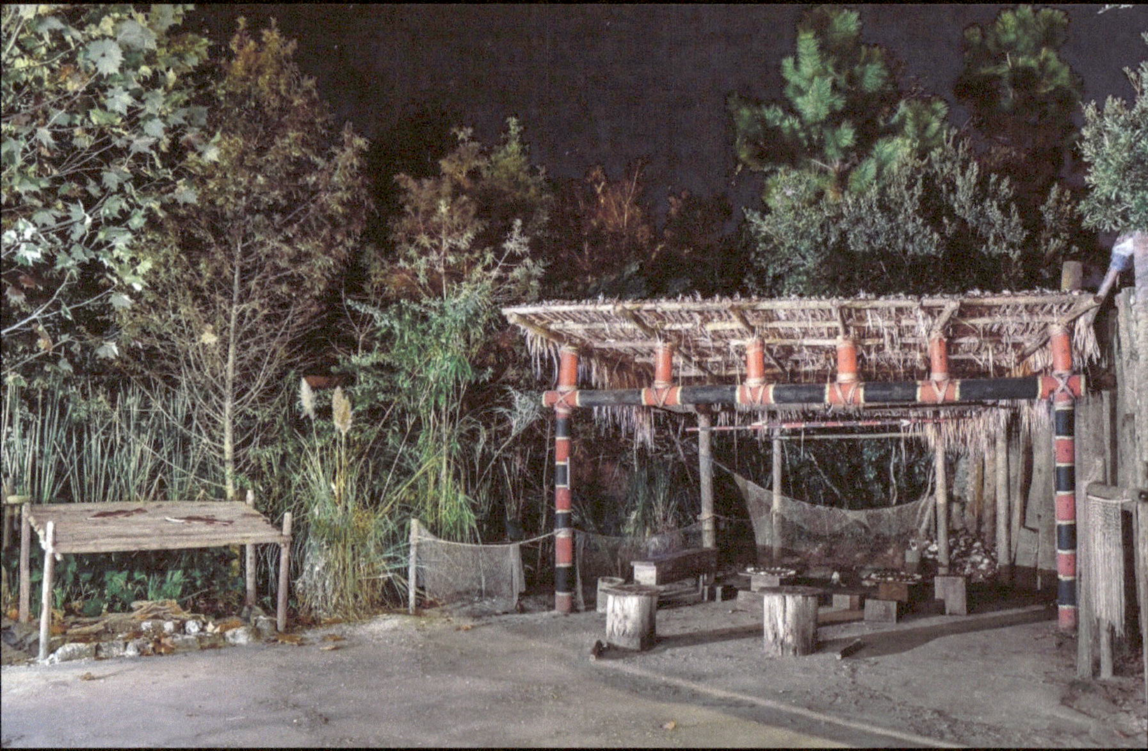

A shot from the Indian village at Fort Menendez.

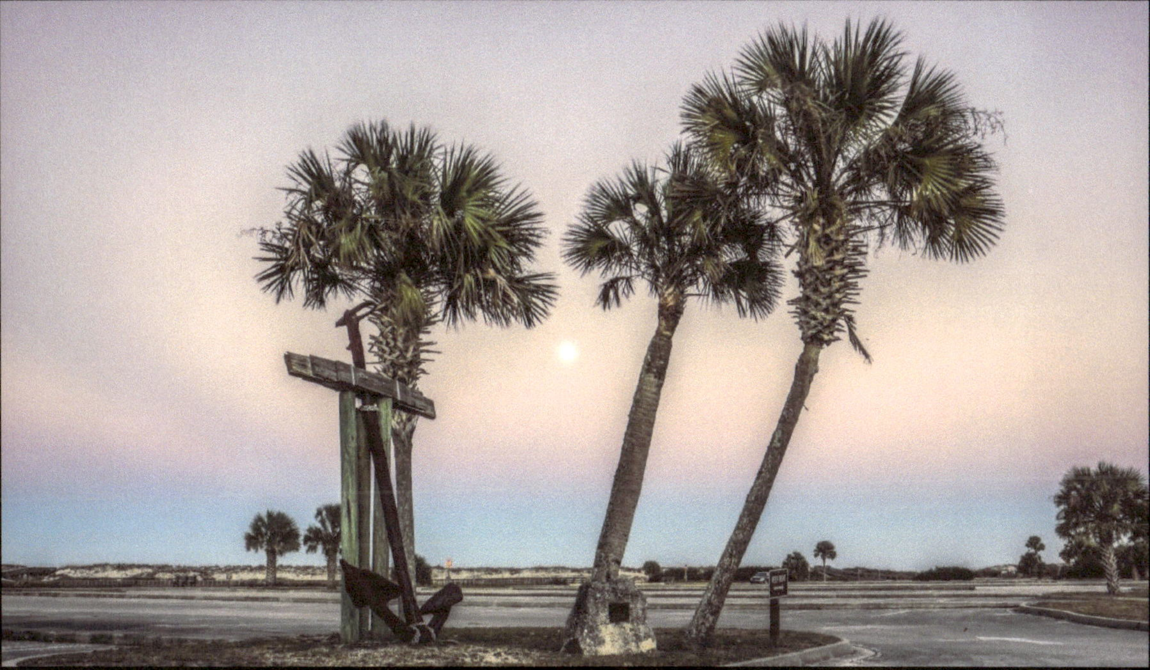

Anastasia State Park

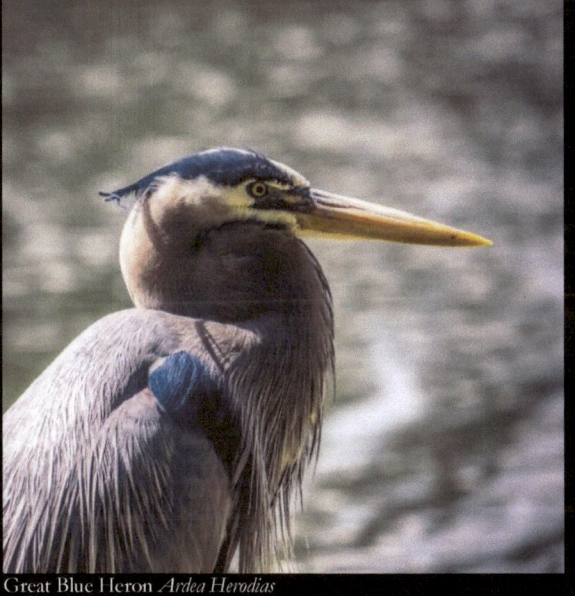

Great Blue Heron *Ardea Herodias*

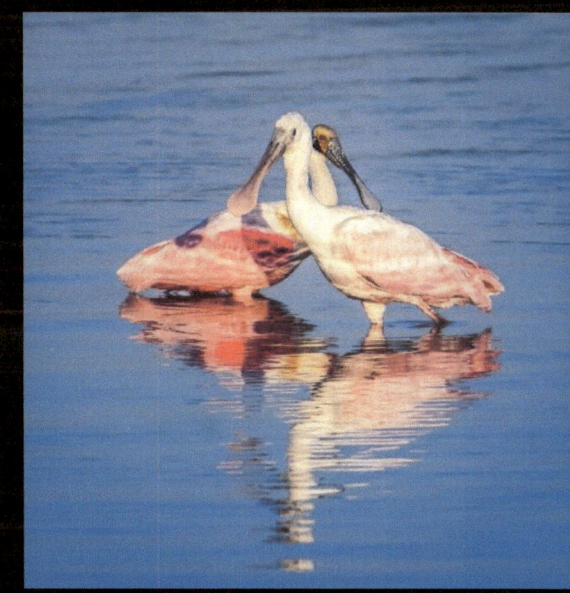

Rosette Spoonbills *Platalea ajaja*

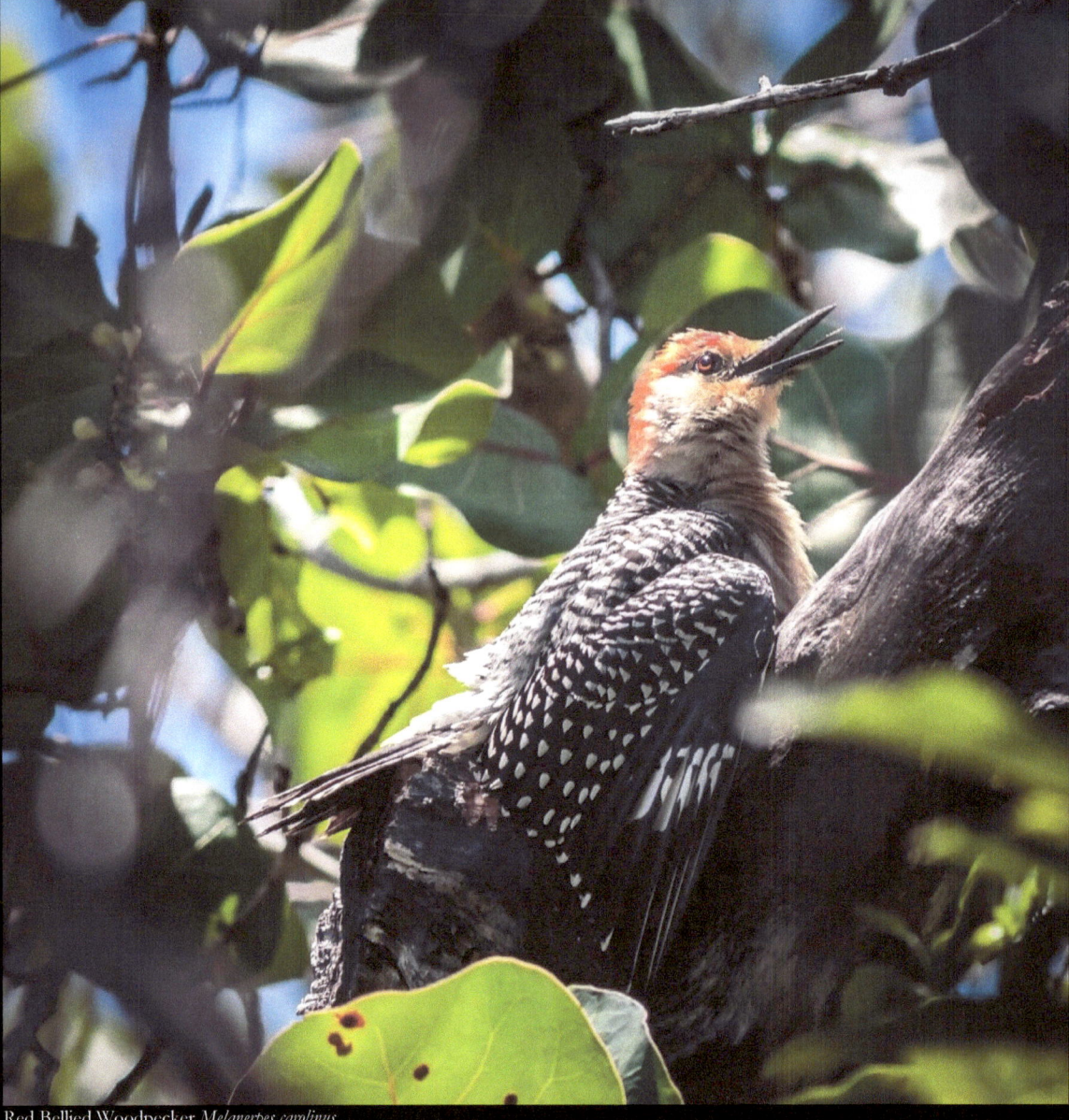

Red Bellied Woodpecker *Melanerpes carolinus*

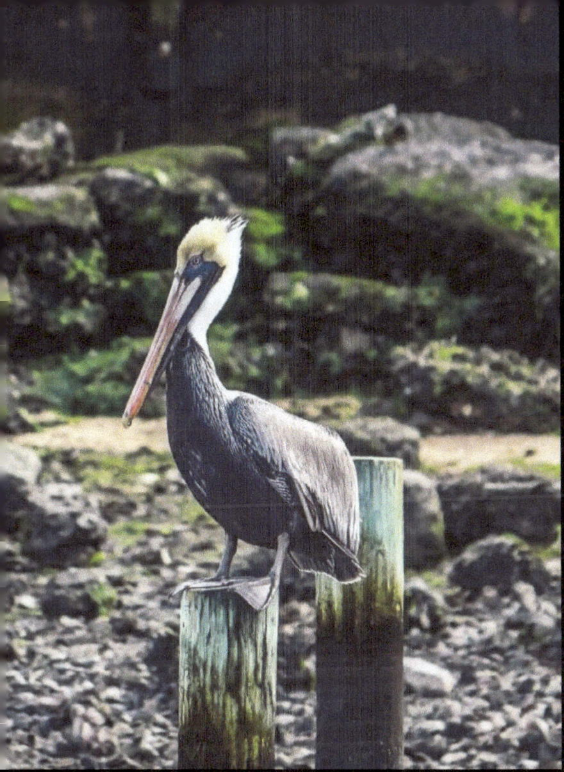

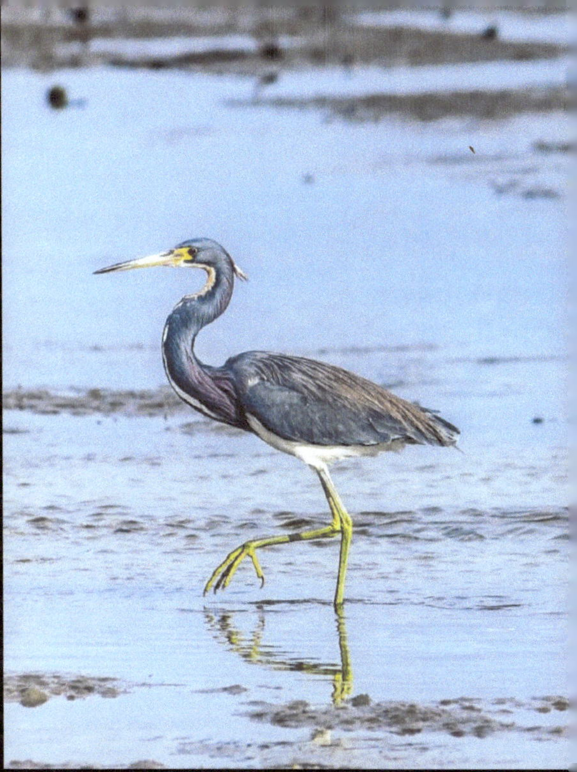

An Eastern Brown Pelican *Pelecanus occidentalis* Tricolored Heron *Egretta tricolor*

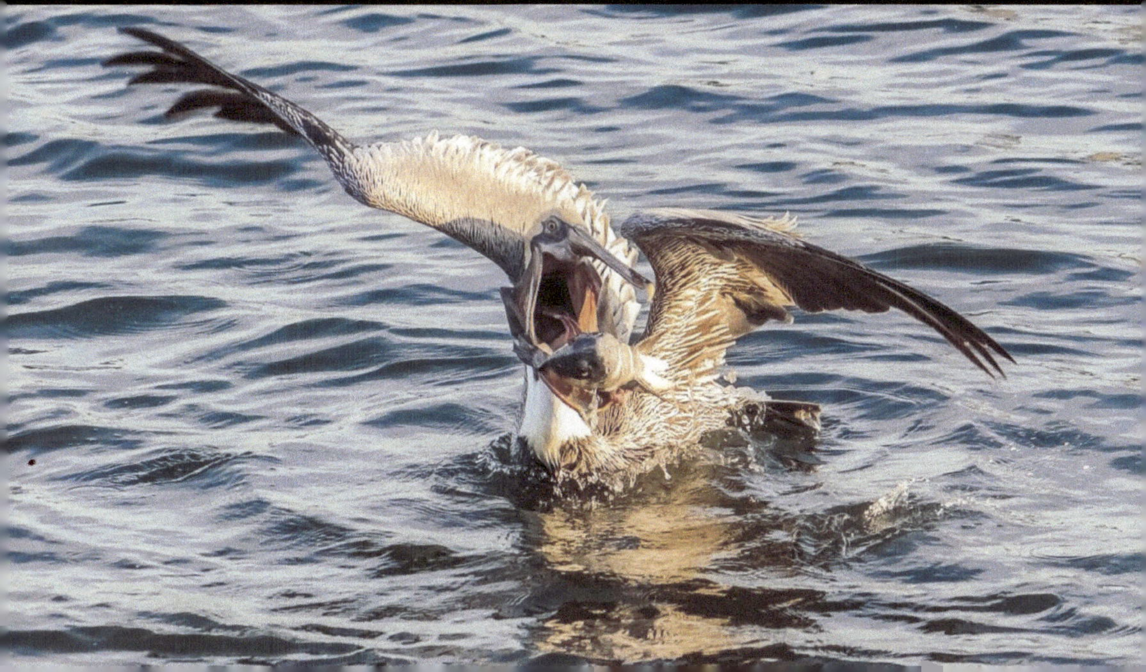

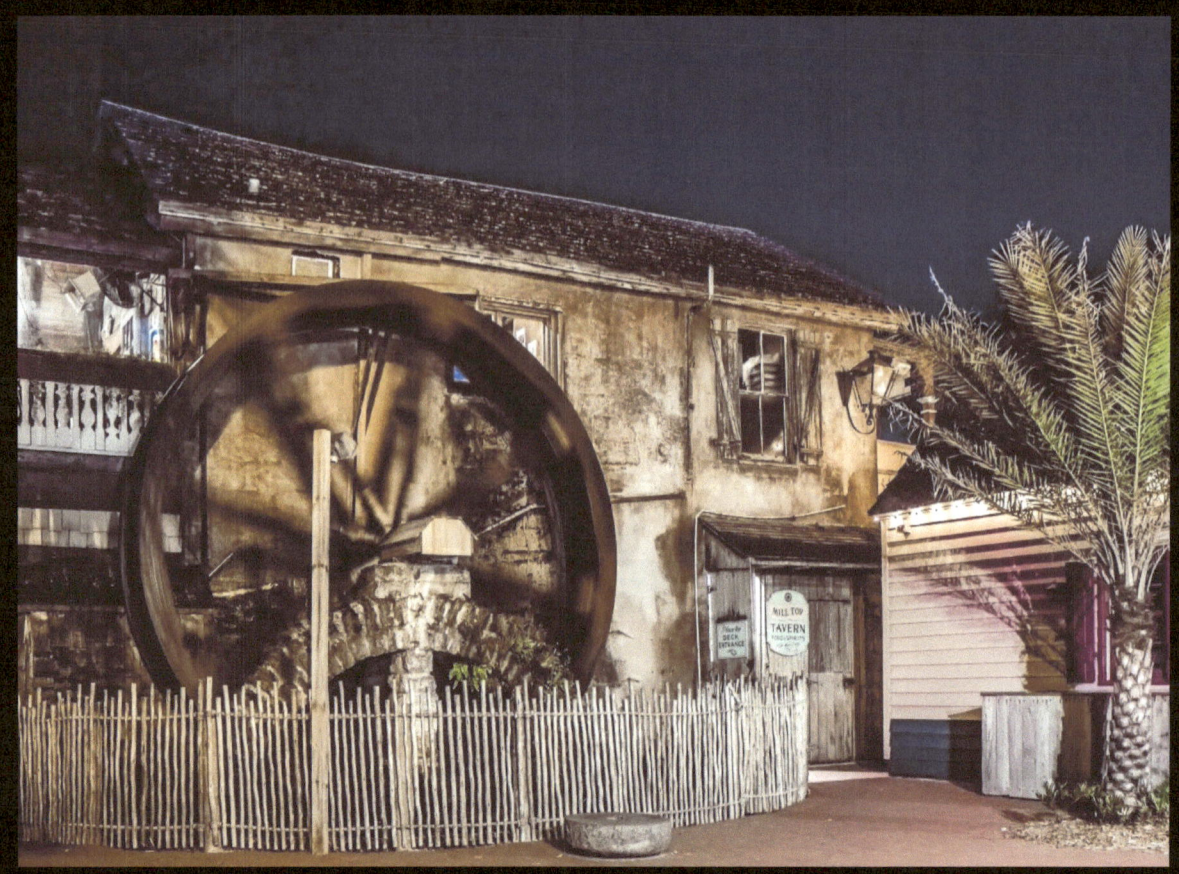

In January 2016, historic Milltop Tavern was set for demolition. After removing the side walls, contractors discovered Coca-Cola and Florida Orange Juice ads that may be almost 100 years old. The building was constructed in the 1880's then converted to a visitor's center in the 1940's. During the conversion, the old signs were covered in stucco and forgotten.

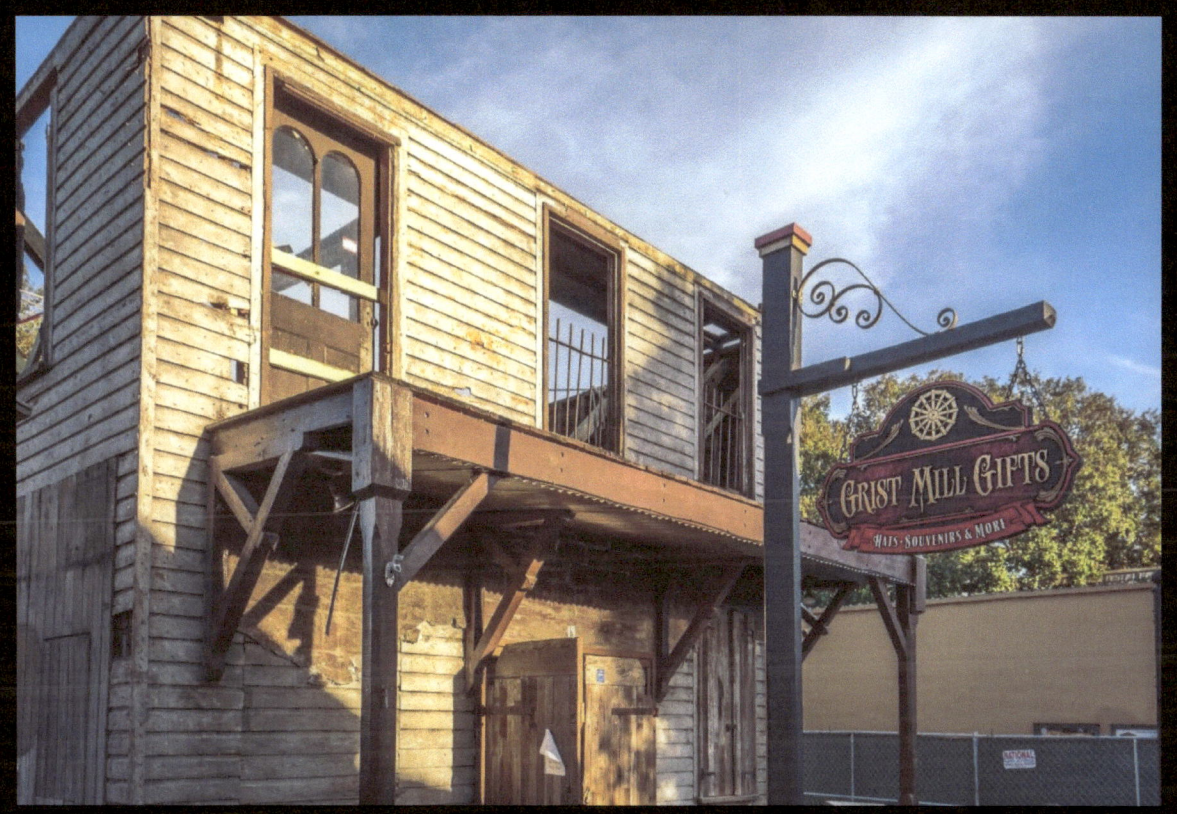

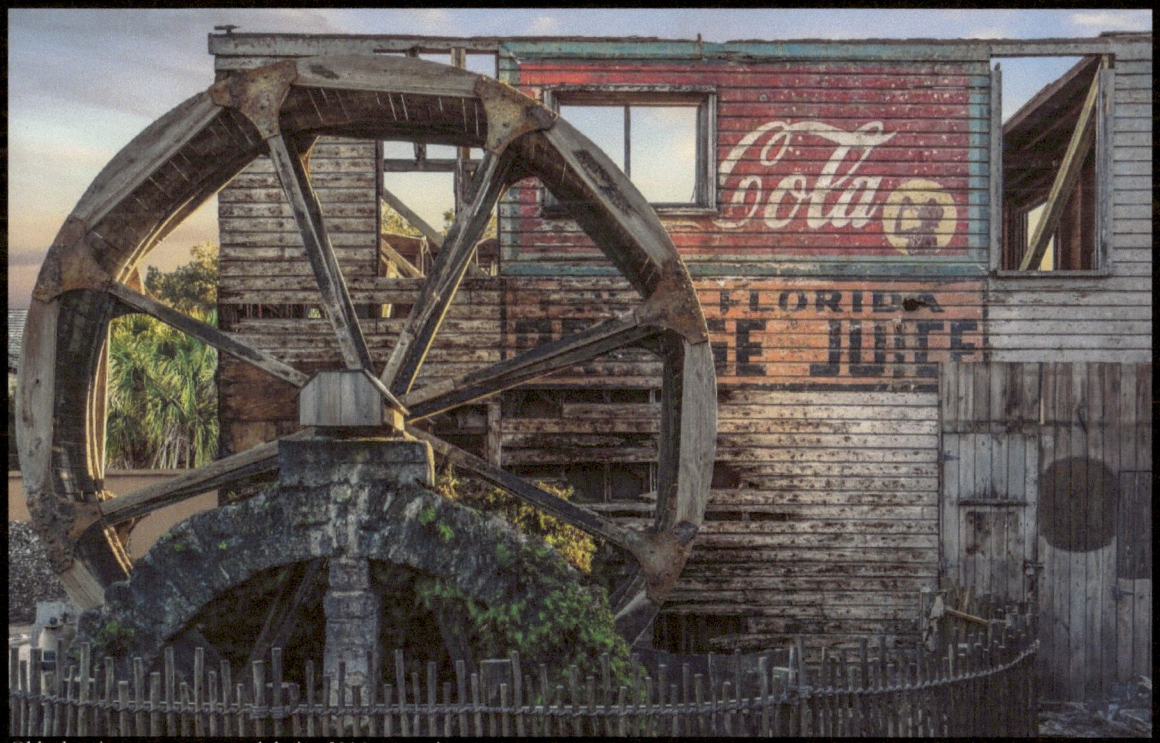

Old advertisements uncovered during 2016 renovations.